Never Give Up!

Linda Bartlett

NEVER ALONE

LINDA BARTLETT

BALBOA.
PRESS
A DIVISION OF HAY HOUSE

Balboa Press books may be ordered through booksellers or by contacting:

Balboa Press
A Division of Hay House
1663 Liberty Drive
Bloomington, IN 47403
www.balboapress.com
1 (877) 407-4847

Because of the dynamic nature of the Internet, any web addresses or links contained in this book may have changed since publication and may no longer be valid. The views expressed in this work are solely those of the author and do not necessarily reflect the views of the publisher, and the publisher hereby disclaims any responsibility for them.

The author of this book does not dispense medical advice or prescribe the use of any technique as a form of treatment for physical, emotional, or medical problems without the advice of a physician, either directly or indirectly. The intent of the author is only to offer information of a general nature to help you in your quest for emotional and spiritual well-being. In the event you use any of the information in this book for yourself, which is your constitutional right, the author and the publisher assume no responsibility for your actions.

Any people depicted in stock imagery provided by Thinkstock are models, and such images are being used for illustrative purposes only.
Certain stock imagery © Thinkstock.

Printed in the United States of America.

ISBN: 978-1-4525-8628-1 (sc)
ISBN: 978-1-4525-8630-4 (hc)
ISBN: 978-1-4525-8629-8 (e)

Library of Congress Control Number: 2013920274

Balboa Press rev. date: 12/17/2013

In honor of my son, Jeffrey.
Thank you for choosing me!

APPRECIATION

There are so many people to thank for this book, so many people who have helped me grow on my own personal journey: my husband, Ken, who has always supported and encouraged me; my daughter, Stephanie, who through her own journey has taught me so very much and who has her own story to share; and, of course, my son, Jeffrey, who, through his life, has opened a whole new world for me.

Thank you, also, to the rest of my loving family and special friends (you know who you are) for paving the path of my journey with your encouragement, fun, and laughter.

And a very special thank-you to the angels for their loving guidance—what a blessing of beauty and peace!

INTRODUCTION

This book has been coming for years. I first started writing the story of my son when he was seven years old. But after a few pages I put it aside, as the right time had not yet come.

Now I know that many new experiences needed to be lived and shared. This book has existed inside me—the sadness, the heartache, the joy, and the love have never gone away. I always believed that I would know when to pick up pen and paper, and after hearing about and witnessing horrific bullying occurring all over this world, I know in my heart that the time has come.

I have been told to look for the gift in the experience. When we can acknowledge that gift, our lives can perhaps gain a deeper meaning and a greater understanding.

As a mother, I wanted to share this story of what it was like to experience life with a child who struggled with physical and mental challenges and intense bullying, because, as I sought wisdom and understanding, I came to experience the beautiful gift of knowing that we are truly never alone.

My son, Jeffrey, also has his own story to share, and I have included an interview with him at the end of this work. He wanted people to learn some of his story in his own words so that perhaps they could identify with the challenges he has endured and know that they, too, can get through the darkest times.

We hope that, as you read these pages, our two perspectives will help you understand that even though people may be different on the outside, on the inside we are the same—beautiful loving souls with hopes and dreams.

If Jeffrey's story can open even a tiny thread of hope, understanding, and love, it is the greatest gift we can give.

PART 1

CHAPTER 1

On February 25, 1975, we began a journey into the unknown. It was a day that forever changed my life. How quickly that incredibly blissful feeling of my tiny baby growing inside me would turn into paralyzing fear.

The day started like any other day, full of hope, anticipation, and love for the small being who was scheduled to enter my world in just over two and a half months. The nursery was prepared: tiny clothes were hanging in the closet, a cuddly teddy bear was waiting to be held, and a rocking chair was ready for beautiful moments that would be shared between a mommy and her special baby. Such joy!

Little did I know that in just a few short hours, the peaceful life that I was living would totally change, and I would begin to walk on a path that was completely foreign to me.

As I sat in the painted yellow rocking chair in my baby's newly decorated nursery, dreamily anticipating the long-awaited time when I would hold my precious baby in my arms, a wrenching pain suddenly thrashed through my swollen body, crashing into my blissful happiness and instantly filling me with pure terror. I was in labor!

No! I had to stop it. It was too soon. *Please, little one, hold on! We need more time. We can stop this. Please, God, we have to stop this!*

I began begging my body to stop the betrayal. I promised anything. I promised not to move. Maybe if I lay perfectly still, my baby could have the necessary time. *If not months, just give us weeks… days.* But that wasn't to be.

Everything became a blur. I was rushed to the hospital and immediately whisked away to a small room, hooked up to ominous-looking machines spewing noises into the air, and then left alone to wait for the unknown.

A wave of intense sadness enveloped me as I lay on the narrow bed and realized that we hadn't decided on a name if our baby was a boy. Tears streamed down my face; this realization just added to the out-of-control feeling as my world continued spiraling downward.

I don't know how long I lay there in such despair. I didn't even hear the door open, but a nurse appeared at my side. Looking into her compassionate eyes, I tearfully told her that my husband and I had chosen a special name for a baby girl but hadn't decided on a name for a baby boy. I pleaded for her to please let my husband come into the room with me just long enough for us to give our baby a name if he was a boy. "Our baby can't be born without a name," I sobbed. As she held my hand while nodding her understanding, she told me that she would bring him in for five minutes so that we could have our time.

In that short five minutes, we tearfully agreed that if we were blessed with a baby boy, his name would be Jeffrey Rowan. And then my husband was gone, and I again lay there all alone in that stark room.

What is happening to my baby? I silently cried out. *Why, oh why, this betrayal of my body?* With wrenching sobs, I willed my body to stop. I pleaded and pleaded and, again, promised anything, but to no avail. I was losing the battle. As I lay there, all alone in that room, my sobs turned into pitiful moans. "I am so sorry, little one. I am so very sorry!"

Suddenly I was rushed down the hall into a brightly lit room full of people moving quickly around me. Why were they yelling—or was I hearing the terrifying screams in my mind? So much commotion, so much tension, as I lay there silently observing.

"Please," I whispered, "please take care of my baby."

And then there was nothing, just a blank space of time, emptiness, and silence.

Where did I go? What did I do? Where was my baby? So many questions left unanswered.

Later, the doctors told me that I had been fully awake during the entire birth of my baby boy, as there wasn't enough time to administer any drugs. Perhaps somewhere in the deep recesses of my mind I was present, but that span of time simply doesn't exist for me, even thirty-eight years later.

Awareness came rushing in as I was thrust back into that cold, bright room. As I cautiously opened my eyes, I saw people in uniforms gathered in one corner, seeming to work furiously; the tension and urgency in the room were so thick that I could hardly breathe.

What was happening? Where was my baby? Why wouldn't someone answer me?

Was I screaming aloud, or was the scream erupting from my being as a soft, pitiful mewling barely leaving my lips? Was that the gut-wrenching sound of me sobbing or simply the sound of my heart shattering?

I heard the loud pounding of footsteps and piercing voices and then doors quickly opened and closed, leaving deafening silence in my world. Although a doctor and nurse stood on the sides of my bed, I was alone. Their lips were moving, but I didn't hear; their hands were touching, but I didn't feel. Their eyes offered sympathy that I didn't see.

Sometime later, I was wheeled to a room where my family anxiously awaited, yet the only one I yearned to see was out of my reach. Loving, compassionate words were spoken, and warm, gentle hugs were given, but I simply couldn't respond. It took too much energy to ask the one question that I was so afraid to ask.

Finally, the door slowly opened, and the doctor quietly approached my bed. I heard the dreaded words: "Your baby is very sick."

Somewhere, far away, the doctor's voice continued. "He has hyaline membrane disease. This is what killed the Kennedy baby."

As I lay there, ensconced again in the following deafening silence, all of a sudden, an overwhelmingly strong force entered my entire body.

Looking into the doctor's kind eyes, I replied, "This is my baby. My baby will live!"

CHAPTER 2

"Oh God, he is so tiny," I whispered as I stood next to the little bed in the Intensive Care Nursery, seeing my baby for the first time. How could they have so many tubes and wires hooked up to such a little body? This was my son, Jeffrey, for whom I had yearned for so long. What had I done? Why had I failed him? Why couldn't I nourish him and continue to provide a safe haven for just a little longer?

Please, oh please, God, don't take him! Please give him the strength to fight! I promise I will do everything I possibly can to help him and protect him. Please trust me with him.

They told me I couldn't hold him, so all I could do was touch him through the wires, constantly telling him how much I loved him and that I always would. He looked so alone and frail, this little baby boy fighting for his life.

"Little one, I will fight with you. Take my strength; let it feed you."

My heart felt as if it were breaking—such heaviness! I wanted so badly to hold him in my arms, to protect him, to take the horrendous hurt away and assure him that I would always take care of him. I wanted to yank those awful wires from his little body, take him in my arms, and run away to a faraway place where nothing could ever harm him again. Yet I knew I could not. Instead, I stood there beside his bed, making promises—so many softly spoken promises—continually shared as he lay there barely breathing.

And so it began, days and nights standing by my premature son—talking to him, incessantly telling him how strong he was, how much Mommy loved him and would never leave him, how God was always with him, and how he would never be alone. This continued day after day, hour after hour, minute after minute, each second a precious gift of time to be cherished.

One morning in that first week, as I was standing by my son's bed touching his tiny body between the wires, the normally efficient hum of the nursery was interrupted.

Oh dear God, what is happening? What do all those alarms mean?

Everyone in the room was running in my direction, pushing past me to get to my baby. Jeffrey's doctor came running through the door, and a nurse appeared next to me, gently yet firmly taking my arm and hurriedly escorting me out of the room.

"No, please, I have to be there with him," I managed to squeak out between lips frozen with fear. Yet I instinctively knew that I would just be in the way. As I slowly stumbled across the room to sit in a corner chair, I bowed my head and prayed for God's knowledge to guide the doctors and nurses as they furiously and tirelessly took care of that little body behind the closed doors.

After what seemed to be hours of agonizing waiting and wondering, afraid to move from that lonely chair, I looked up to see the doctor striding over to me, his eyes looking tired and bloodshot.

"His lungs had collapsed. He couldn't breathe. We didn't have time to rush him to surgery, so I immediately inserted a tube into his chest in order to allow the fluid to drain. The next twenty-four hours should tell us if the procedure was successful."

I sat frozen in the chair that had become my refuge. I was aware of what was being said to me, yet I simply could not comprehend the meaning. I could not give in to the chilling fear that was enveloping my body like a dark, leaden cloak weighing heavily on my spirit. Numbness seeped into my pores.

I willed my body to move, one step at a time, dreading to see even more tubes and wires in my precious little one, yet knowing that I had to get to him, to gently touch him, to let him hear my words of love, to infuse my strength into his little body.

He was so very tiny, and he had already been through so much in such a short time. I didn't want him to hurt, but I just couldn't let him go. He had to know how much I loved him and wanted him. I didn't know if he could hear me, but I prayed that somewhere in his mind and spirit he could hear and feel my presence, that he could know how much I loved him, and that he could feel my strength.

As the minutes at his side turned into hours, I could feel my legs slowly beginning to fold as complete exhaustion viciously attacked my body.

I could no longer pretend. I was totally depleted. One of the nurses approached me and gently led me down the hall back to my room, tucking me into bed while assuring me that she would personally stay with my baby the rest of the night. I was too exhausted to even form the words to thank her, and as my head lay down on the pillow, I immediately drifted off to a blissful place where no conscious thoughts could penetrate.

CHAPTER 3

Early the next morning, as the sun made its appearance, tentatively peeking over the horizon, I was once again standing at my son's side, thanking God for another day. I had become accustomed to all of the tubes and wires and the whirring of the machines, and I marveled at my tiny little fighter. Every breath taken was a victory! One by one, I counted them as I continued to talk to my special little one, telling him over and over how strong he was and how much I loved him.

And so the day went, hour after hour after hour. Nurses came and went; doctors came and went; all encouraged me to go to my room for some much-needed rest. But I simply could not. I could not leave him alone as long as I had the strength to stand and the voice to talk.

A tiny glimpse of hope began to appear as the hours slowly ticked away. I had to stay positive for Jeffrey's sake. I instinctively knew that at a later date I would absorb the severity of what was happening, but for now, any negative doubts and fears simply had to stay at a far distance. They could not creep into this protective bubble I had created for my son.

Eventually, a kind nurse enveloped me in her arms, and she gently escorted me back to my room, all the while speaking soft, soothing words. I was so beyond tired that I could no longer resist her gentle prodding. And, although her words could not penetrate the thick fog, it felt good to just let someone else take charge, even for a short while.

After a brief rest, I hurriedly made my way back down that now familiar hall with renewed energy, only to be blocked from entering the Intensive Care Nursery where my baby lay. A doctor was working on one of the babies, I was told, so no one could go into the room. Once again, I sat in the lonely chair with eyes focused on the swinging doors, fervently hoping and praying that they weren't speaking of the doctor I knew—the doctor I had come to know and love for taking care of my son. I berated myself for leaving him while I rested.

What seemed like an eternity passed before the doors swung open, allowing a now familiar face to walk through, shoulders somewhat slumped as he slowly came toward me. Kind sympathetic eyes looked at me as he proceeded to tell me that my baby had started breathing on his own earlier, so the breathing machine had been unhooked and set nearby. He continued to explain that it was critical for him to be off the machine as soon as possible in order to prevent other long-term health issues, but, after only a few short breaths, his lungs collapsed again.

Thankfully, his doctor had been near the hospital. (Coincidence? I think not.) Another surgery was performed, again inserting a tube into that tiny little chest, allowing the lungs to drain—another emergency surgery that had to be performed right at Jeffrey's bed in the Intensive Care Nursery.

Tears were dried up as I hurriedly made my way back to my baby, and as I saw the big machine with all the tubes and wires breathing for my little one, my heart physically ached. Oh, how I wanted to pick him up, tubes, wires, and all and just hold him! I yearned to protect him from all that pain and fear, yet I couldn't. I felt so helpless as I took his tiny hand in mine, for that was all I could do.

What was he thinking? To think that this little soul was suffering so much was almost more than I could bear. I begged to change places with him. I wanted to make it all better, to assure him that his life on this earthly realm would be a great one. We had to believe that; we just had to believe that! I knew that the greatest gift I could give him at that point was just pure love and boundless strength. If he could not breathe on his own, then he would have every bit of strength I had to help him. He would know what astounding love was surrounding him now and awaiting him in his future. He would know that he was not alone and that we could do this together. He must know and feel those things!

I vowed that I would not leave his side again. After all, look what happened the last time I left to get some rest. Was I thinking rationally? Absolutely not! And as the hours ticked away and the stars filled the sky, I vaguely came to the realization that I was doing my little one a disservice. It was time for me to practice what I had shared with others over the years. If I didn't take care of myself, how could I possibly be here to take care of him? So easy to say; so hard to do!

Finally, when the numbers on the clock began to blur and my words became such an effort to even come out of my mouth, I knew that I had no choice but to get some rest for the next day. And as I slowly stumbled down the hall, literally telling myself to put one foot in front of the other, I fell into my bed and was instantly in a totally exhausted sleep.

CHAPTER 4

Early the next morning, as I drifted back into consciousness, I immediately knew that something was terribly wrong.

Oh, dear God, what has happened to me? I silently cried as I realized that I was bleeding. I didn't know what was going on, and I didn't have the energy to care. I didn't have the strength to talk; I didn't have the strength to walk. I could barely move. I couldn't think. There was just nothing: no thoughts, no words, just nothing—a blank canvas.

A little while later, the phone in my room rang, but I couldn't talk, so it just continued to ring and ring. Family and friends came into my room, trying to engage in conversation. I heard, yet I didn't. I simply stared into nothingness.

The doctor was notified as I continued to lie in my bed totally listless. One nurse who had been taking care of my baby all night came to my room to report on his progress; she knew something was terribly wrong for me not to be with him.

I listened, but I couldn't comprehend what she was saying. I simply lay there, an empty lifeless shell. And so the day continued.

Evidently word spread among my very close friends who were attending a special symposium based on love and understanding that weekend. The phone again rang. My new roommate answered it and reached out to me, phone in her hand. I barely turned my head. My arms couldn't move.

After saying something to the person on the other end, who happened to be my very dearest male friend, she got out of her bed and crossed the room to put the phone to my ear. To this day, I have no idea what he said.

My friend was running the symposium that weekend, so a short while later some other dear friends who had been at the symposium came into my room and began talking to me about my baby: how I had to let him go if he needed to, and trust that God would take care of him.

No, I thought, *I don't want to listen!* I hated the words they were speaking. They didn't understand.

Just leave me alone! It hurts too much to hear. It hurts too much to feel. I can't let him go. How can I do that? Please just go away and let me go back to nothingness.

Then, as I looked into their incredibly loving eyes, I began to hear wrenching sobs erupting from deep crevices within my body. They wouldn't stop; they just kept coming and coming. My friends held me like a baby and rocked me as I continued to woefully sob, moaning that I couldn't let him go—I just couldn't!

Suddenly the most incredible peace enveloped me, pouring into every pore of my body the most amazing, all-consuming sense of pure love, unlike anything I had ever experienced. My entire body instantly filled with this intensifying energy, and without thinking, I jumped out of bed and flew down the hall, feet barely touching the floor; the medical staff stared at me with open mouths.

Someone called my name, but I was on a mission. I was going to my son! He was waiting for me.

As I entered the Intensive Care Nursery, I quickly moved to the little bed in the far left side of the room. There he was, lying so still, tubes and wires everywhere. Such a tiny soul lay on that bed, eyes closed, little chest barely moving up and down as he struggled for air.

As I continued to watch my baby struggle, I knew what I had to do.

Oh God, this is so hard, so incredibly painful! Yet I had to let him go. He couldn't stay here just for me if he needed to go. I had to make him understand that Mommy would be okay, that I would forever love him, and that it was okay if he needed to leave. He was such a brave little fighter, and I understood if he was tired of that fight. I had to set him free. The words, "Let go and let God," resonated in my mind and heart.

And as I wrapped his tiny little hand around my finger, we had our talk, just the two of us. I told him how he was surrounded by angels, how God was always with him and that he was not alone. He would never be alone. It was his choice now, and he must make it freely. I would always love him in a very special place in my heart, whatever his choice was.

Then I turned around and walked back down the hall to my room knowing that, as much as it hurt, I would be okay; I, too, was not alone.

One of the nurses followed me back to my room and gently helped me get back into my bed, saying that she had called the doctor about the excessive bleeding and was told that he was in surgery, but he would come by to check on me afterward.

She also said that I needed to stay in bed until the doctor arrived.

She then examined me because she was concerned that I might have caused more bleeding, only to discover that it had stopped completely. The look of puzzlement on her face was priceless; she just shook her head and left my room.

How was it that I could just jump out of bed and practically run down the hall, when all day I couldn't even move or respond to anyone? And, more importantly, how could the heavy bleeding just suddenly stop?

I was later told by the doctor that, medically speaking, there were no answers, as these things just don't happen. But spiritually, I knew: a miracle had occurred. I also knew what decision my baby had made. He would stay here with me. He would continue to fight, as he had a mission, a purpose, to fulfill on this planet Earth.

What I didn't know at that point until one of my son's nurses later came to my room, was that he had almost left several times that morning—the same time period that I was shutting down. He would totally stop breathing, alarms would sound, and nurses would run over to get him stimulated again. Finally, one nurse stood by his bed her entire shift "tickling" his tiny feet to keep him breathing.

Yes, my son was "checking out" at the very same time I was. We had been leaving together, and we both ultimately made our decisions to stay. Coincidence or miracle? I choose to believe miracle!

The very next morning, tubes and wires began to be removed one by one from his tiny body, and he was gently moved to an incubator across the room where he would stay an additional six weeks. He finally was breathing on his own for the first time since he had come into this world.

What a glorious day to see my little one for the first time free of so many tubes and wires! And when the nurse gleefully asked me if I would like to hold my baby, my heart just grew with sheer joy and happiness. To actually be able to hold him in my arms and cuddle him was the greatest moment.

I couldn't get enough time with him. I just wanted to stop the clock and hold him endlessly. He was still so very tiny, but now at last he could physically feel my love for him emanating from my entire being. And as I looked into his eyes, I saw such a beautiful old soul, and I knew without a doubt that there would be an incredible journey ahead of us—a journey that we would take together. And I, again, vowed that I would love him and protect him with every fiber of my being.

And so it began. Each day was a celebration of each little accomplishment: a soft mewling cry, the first tentative suck from a preemie nipple, tiny arms and legs moving, those precious ounces gained, and eventually outgrowing the Barbie-like preemie diapers— each was such a tremendous accomplishment to be cherished.

Approximately seven weeks from the time Jeffrey entered this world, I heard the glorious words that I had so yearned for. I could take him home with me the next day. I was at once both ecstatic and terrified. I would finally be able to take care of my baby, but what if I did something wrong? I didn't know anything about taking care of and nourishing a tiny baby. After all, he wasn't even five pounds. What if he went through all of that pain and struggling, only to have his own mommy unintentionally harm him? The doubts and fears came rushing at me with a vengeance as I prayed for strength and guidance.

CHAPTER 5

As the months passed, I celebrated each accomplishment, regardless of how large or small. But I was always on alert, seeing—but not wanting to see—telltale signs.

I spent much of my time in denial. Yes, I had heard the doctor tell me that my son had cerebral palsy as a result of his premature birth and that he would face many challenges in life. Yes, I had listened when I was told that the levels of oxygen that had to be administered to him while in the hospital would affect his eyes and that the constant high-pitched sound of the oxygen filling his enclosed isolette, after finally being able to get off the breathing machine with all its wires, would cause some hearing loss. I realized that my son didn't sit up, crawl, or walk when "the books" said babies should. But I simply would not accept those facts. I was always searching for answers, carting his ever-growing medical files from one doctor to another, only to be told the same thing time after time. "If I had seen these medical records without seeing your son, medically speaking, I would say there is no way he could have survived, and if he did, there is no way he could ever walk or talk or function for himself. He is a miracle to even be here."

Miracle, indeed, but the rest were words, only words. I would not, could not, accept them. There had to be an answer somewhere. I just had to keep searching. After all, I had promised my baby that I would always protect him. I could not and would not stop!

My days were filled with endless searching, inwardly begging for the "right" answer, the words that would say that my child would be okay, that my child would live a normal life, just a small glimmer of hope, a tiny crumb, anything to grab on to. But sadly that never came. Those words were never spoken.

And so the searching continued—doctor after doctor after doctor—only to walk away each of the countless times with even more determination that I would find the answer. There had to be a path for us, somewhere, somehow, someone.

Meanwhile, I was always looking for signs, any little thing to feed my heart, this heart that loved so much, that wanted so much for my little one. I never accepted the medical facts. After all, he was my miracle child. He had fought so very hard to survive, why couldn't he walk? Why couldn't he talk? Why couldn't he laugh and play and read and write? We would just simply try harder—and so we did.

As I continued my searching journey, I visualized an absolutely frantic gerbil or hamster in a huge maze, running as fast as it's little legs could go, constantly trying to find that open door while bumping into wall after wall after wall, yet never stopping, never, never giving up.

Inner strength is such a marvelous phenomenon! Where does it come from? How does it replenish when, at the end of the day, this body vessel is so completely drained? Inner strength put the smile on my face for the world to see, the melodious sound of laughter for the world to hear, the continuous motion of putting one foot down and then the other, and the joy of life in moment after moment—inner strength, never ending.

CHAPTER 6

During Jeffrey's nine-month checkup, his doctor said that he wanted to immediately order an MRI. He was concerned about possible pressure building in his head, and he wanted to rule out either a growth or a leakage. As he described the procedure—emphasizing how totally still Jeff would have to be in the machine and during the entire process—I questioned how it could happen. He was just a baby. I was told that he would be given something to calm him but that he had to be awake the entire time.

I wanted so badly to just put my head in the sand and take my baby away: no more machines, no more doctors, no more hospitals, no more pain, no more fear. Yet I knew that wasn't the answer. We had to know what we were dealing with, and whatever it was, we would face it together.

As I held my child in my arms, rocking him to sleep the night before the procedure, I again prayed that he would be protected, and I asked God to send his angels to please surround him with their loving, healing energy. I also asked for an abundance of strength when I handed him to someone else, as I was told that I would not be able to be with him. As I gently put him in his crib, my tears falling freely onto his little face, I knew that I would stay the entire night just to be near him.

As the sun again peeked over the horizon, bringing with it a new day, I tiptoed out of his nursery with a heavy heart. Within the hour we would be at the hospital, where someone would give him calming medicine and, later, take him out of my arms. I imagined my hot, steaming shower as a spray of golden white light pouring over my body with its gentle healing strength; I again knew that my son and I were not alone.

The medicine was given as I held Jeff in my arms; I was told that they would come back for him in about half an hour. That way he would get drowsy while I was holding him, hopefully alleviating trauma. However, when they came back to get him, he was still wide awake and alert. I asked them to please let me be with him, but I was told again that it was against hospital policy, although we could have a little more time for the medicine to take effect. They had read his chart and were aware of the trauma he had already endured in his short life.

What seemed like only minutes later, they returned to the waiting room to take my son, only to find that he was still completely alert. I was told that they couldn't wait any longer to administer the procedure because the doctor was anxious to get the results, so they gently took him from my arms and hurriedly walked through the doors with my son's cries piercing the air.

My arms were so empty and my heart was so sad as I was again separated from my baby. Complete numbness took over my body as I stood there looking at those closed doors.

An eternity passed, or so it seemed, when I heard Jeff's cries getting louder. The doors opened, and there he was, his little arms reaching out to me, tears rolling down his face. As I quickly took him into my arms where he belonged, those pitiful cries subsided. He was safe.

They hadn't been able to get him to lie still. Imagine, a little, terrified baby surrounded by strangers while being put into a giant tube! I was told that they wouldn't be able to perform the procedure.

Oh no, this wouldn't happen! If Jeffrey's doctor felt it was imperative that this procedure be done, then it would be done, and it would be done the right way! I had no doubt that as long as I was with my baby—holding his little hand, touching him, and talking to him the entire time—we could do this.

I convinced them to just let me try (I think they knew that I wouldn't leave). I'm certain that they were simply humoring me, thinking that it was totally absurd that a mother could do this with positive results, but I wasn't taking no for an answer. We had tried their way with their crazy rules; now we were doing it my way.

The test began, and my little son was hearing my loving words and feeling my strength and my touch as he was put into that big machine far enough to get the images they needed of his head. I never let go of Jeffrey's little hand, and I never stopped talking as I stood as close to him as I possibly could.

Did he move? Not even a tiny wiggle! Did he cry? Not even a whimper! My little angel lay perfectly still the entire time.

The medical staff were absolutely amazed. They later shared that they could hardly believe what they had seen: the incredible loving bond and trust between a baby and a parent, an understanding strong and intense. They would never have believed it if they had not seen it with their own eyes.

I hope that they took that experience with them the next time they started to separate a child from his or her parent!

When I shared with Jeff's doctor what had happened at the hospital, he simply smiled, shook his head, and said, "Such a tiny miracle child. There's so much more than the medical world." And as he gave us the good news that there was nothing to cause pressure inside my baby's head, we both rejoiced. Another milestone! Each positive accomplishment was like the tallest majestic mountain reaching up to the sky.

In the months that followed, each day was a celebration of life, being aware of the beautiful vibrant colors of flowers, the soothing sound of water as it slowly trickled over pebbles in a calming stream, the soft blades of grass as they gently tickled my baby's feet, and, oh, that magnificent sound of laughter that bubbled up from my son as he reached out to experience life. I was learning to live in the present and to be thankful for the moments, storing each one in a memory bank to draw from at a later time.

CHAPTER 7

A few months after Jeff's MRI, his doctor encouraged me to take him to an eye specialist. So after joyfully celebrating his first birthday, I reluctantly made the appointment. It had to be done, but oh, how I yearned for him to just be able to play and laugh like a child should. I knew deep down that we were about to experience another roller-coaster ride, with dips so low that they would take my breath away, and I was already anticipating the rough, slow climb back up.

After spending another sleepless night watching my son, reflecting back on the first year of his life, I walked into the doctor's office with a brave front, knowing that we could get through whatever we had to; yet deep inside I was a completely terrified little girl.

"Your son's eyes have been damaged from the amount of oxygen that he had to have in order to survive when he was so sick. He needs to have surgery immediately to correct his eye muscles and his sight."

I wasn't surprised as I heard him speak, yet I just wanted to scream. Not his eyes. Not another hospital and not more pain. The thought of him being taken from me again was haunting. Why couldn't we just run away where no one could ever find us; where no one could ever hurt my baby again? Those thoughts didn't make sense, but life just didn't make sense. It was so hard, and it seemed that when we would finally get a little bit of a reprieve to enjoy the warm rays of sunshine, the tumultuous storms would come to knock us down again.

As much as I wanted to, I just couldn't stop time. So the day that I had dreaded arrived way too quickly. There we were, in the hospital, as I sat holding my little one in my arms, watching the minutes, the seconds, on the clock ticking away, bringing the moment closer when someone would once again take him out of my arms.

Although he was supposed to be drowsy from the medicine that had been injected into his IV, he was wide awake. He was fighting again. Why did his life have to be so difficult? He was just an innocent little child.

Loving, soothing words were spoken, assuring him that God and his angels were surrounding him and that he would soon be back with his mommy. Silently, I was praying to transfer my strength to him yet again.

Then they took him and scurried down the hall; Jeffrey was holding both little arms out for me and screaming, *"Mommy, Mommy!"* His cries pierced my heart.

Oh, how I wanted to run down that hall and grab him out of the arms that held him. Those should have been my arms holding him and comforting him. Yet my arms were empty. I simply had to stand there, crumbling inside, as he disappeared behind yet another set of closing doors.

How long did it take? I don't know. All I know is that while he was in surgery, I was there with him. Time, as we know it, stopped. Yes, my physical body was waiting in the chair, but I was gone. I was with my child.

A nurse was standing in front of me, saying something as I returned. "Your son came out of anesthesia very quickly, and he is crying for you. We haven't been able to calm him. Do you want to go to him in recovery?"

As she was finishing her question, I started running down the hall. All I could think of was that my son was alone and scared—and this time he was in total darkness! I had to get to him as quickly as I possibly could.

I heard his cries as I burst through those doors. *"Mommy, Mommy!"* And there he was—that precious little body with both eyes bandaged, so scared, so terribly scared.

Please give me the strength to get through this. Please show me what to do. Please give me the words to reach my son. God, please surround us with Your healing love. Angels, please protect us.

"It's okay, baby. Mommy's here." With the sound of those words, he turned his head toward me and immediately stopped crying; I picked him up and held him in my arms, consoling him with constant words of how strong he was, how much I loved him, and how God and the angels were always protecting him—all familiar words that he had heard before.

And that is how we sat for the next few hours—surrounded by nurses taking care of patients, with orders being given and machines whirring in response—yet somehow we were alone, just the two of us, my baby resting in my arms, his little head with bandaged eyes ensconced in total darkness.

I never left his side. Yes, people tried to get me to go home, even for a few hours, to get some rest; loving friends wanted to stay with him while I slept. All had good intentions and were appreciated, but they just didn't understand. I had to be with him at all times. I had to be there to constantly comfort him and to constantly reassure him that I would be there when he woke. There was total darkness in his world. He couldn't see, but he could hear my words. He couldn't see, but he could feel my body as I held him against me, showering him with my love.

This continued even after we were able to go home. I was with my child constantly while he lived in his dark world.

Finally, the day arrived when the bandages would be removed. We went to the doctor's office that morning, and as I held Jeff in my lap, I prayed that he would be able to see his world again—that fun and laughter would fill our days as he would be able to continue to experience new wonders.

I sat, anxiously anticipating the bandages finally being removed; I was fearful of the outcome! So many mixed emotions churned inside me, but then a slow, tentative smile spread across his precious little mouth, and one word soared me to great heights as he looked at me and softly said, "Mommy."

Big tears of joy, thankfulness, relief, and happiness freely cascaded down my face as I held my special little boy. Jeffrey could see!

CHAPTER 8

Everyday life continued with both little and big celebrations along the way. As Jeffrey celebrated his third birthday, loving the icing on his cake, he was progressing in his development. He was such a happy little boy with the most beautiful smile. He loved playing with cars, and he would race them down the hallway, laughing hilariously when they would crash against the walls. And, yes, he was talking, walking, and even riding his cherished blue tricycle.

He was also very excited about his baby sister, who was in his mommy's tummy. He wanted to share his toys with her. And although he still had to go to doctors frequently for his eyes, his hearing, and his general development because of his cerebral palsy, our home was filled with wondrous laughter, which we cherished.

On Sunday, May 28, 1978, our beautiful baby daughter was born, and as I held her in my arms for the first time, my entire being was filled with joy and love. Our family was complete, and I thanked God for entrusting me with two of His precious children.

Jeff was thrilled with his baby sister (even though he tried to flush her little silver brush down the toilet), and he loved helping me take care of her. Life was great, and I was so thankful.

A while later, after deciding to build a new home, we sold our existing house and moved temporarily into an apartment until our new home was completed. I remember being in the small kitchen one day, preparing an early dinner, when all of a sudden Jeffrey came running into the room, his little body trembling. I looked into eyes full of fear, and I immediately stopped what I was doing, scooped him up into my arms, and carried him to the sofa, holding him close to my body.

As I continued to hold him, rocking him ever so gently, he told me in a shaky, scared little voice, "Mommy, the lights. The lights are so big, and they scare me. I'm afraid, Mommy."

Instantly, I knew that he was talking about his time in the Intensive Care Nursery, where he had spent the first seven weeks of his life.

How did I know? I can't answer that, but I did, and I didn't question it. I asked Jeffrey to show me the lights. As we walked into his room hand in hand, he looked up, and said, "There, Mommy. Those lights. They scare me."

As I stood there and gazed around his room, with the sunshine peeking through the windows, I saw no lights, not even one. And yet I didn't doubt even for a second that my little one did indeed see his scary lights. I also knew what those lights were: those super bright lights that were always on day and night in the room where my baby had fought so hard to live.

It was imperative that I help him face that fear and understand it so that he could, hopefully, let it go. As we sat on the floor of his room, his little body encircled in the safety of my arms, I explained what the lights were. I told him that he had been sick when he was born, and he had stayed in a room with big bright lights while he got better. I told him how he was loved from the very beginning and how that love grew every day while he got stronger and stronger, until he got so healthy and strong that he was able to leave those lights behind and come home. I told him how proud we were of him for fighting so hard.

He then looked up into my eyes and said, "Mommy, they hurt me. Those people hurt me. The lights were so big. Mommy, I was so scared."

As I sat there holding my precious little boy, I knew that he was remembering those first few weeks of his life—those days and weeks when he was hooked up to machines so he could breathe; when he was constantly poked with needles to check his oxygen level so he wouldn't totally lose his sight; when his little lungs collapsed not once, but twice; and when his doctor cut into his tiny chest to insert a tube, right there in that room with the bright lights. Those big bright lights were where people hurt him.

Together we sat in his room, looking at the "lights," until finally he turned his head toward me and said, with a big beautiful smile on his face, "It's okay now, Mommy. The lights are gone. I'm not afraid."

I continued to hold him. I couldn't let him see me unsuccessfully fighting back tears of sorrow for this little soul who had endured so much pain and fear in such a short time in his life. I also shed tears of gratitude as I thanked God for giving me the strength and the insight to know how to help him through his terrifying experience so that he could understand it and, hopefully, begin to heal.

What a tremendous lesson that was for me as we continued our journey—how critical it is that we all understand that, even as a tiny newborn, we are aware of our surroundings. From the very beginning of life on this earth, we store memories that can, and do, affect us in later years. Perhaps with understanding and acknowledgment, our fears and hurts will begin to dissipate so that we don't have to carry them into other realms of our lives.

CHAPTER 9

Days turned into months and months into a few years, and then it was time for Jeffrey to interact in a school setting with other children, at least for a few hours each day. I think all, or at least most, parents are somewhat nervous about that first experience for our children in a totally new environment. I know that I was extremely apprehensive about how he would be accepted. For instance, because of the cerebral palsy, he couldn't walk with the same easy gait as other children. He couldn't run as fast or with ease. It was very difficult for him to sit on a floor. He couldn't hear well, especially when there were other noises or if more than one person was talking at the same time. Although his vision was much improved after his surgery, it was still somewhat difficult for him to see from a distance. He simply wasn't the rough and tough, carefree three-and-a-half-year-old little boy.

Yes, I was very nervous about the beginning of his school days, and at the same time, I was really excited about him having friends to play with and about him learning new things. Of course, he only saw my excitement.

After extensive research and many interviews, I decided on a religious preschool, hoping and believing that they would be cognizant of my son's challenges and hardships. Leaving him that first day was really tough for me, but he seemed to adapt, and as I slowly walked away, he was playing with another little boy.

I was ecstatic thinking he had been accepted and could laugh and play for a few hours a day. But after a couple of weeks, I received a call from the school saying that they needed to meet with me regarding my son. I asked them if he was okay, to which they replied yes, but they said they would rather talk with me in person, so we made an appointment for the next morning.

When I got to the school, I took Jeffrey to his class as usual, and he immediately ran up to a little boy and started playing. I was so happy to see that, but I didn't have a good feeling about the meeting. However, I was shocked when they told me the reason for the call. Jeffrey wouldn't color when the children were supposed to color. *Color?* They were concerned because he wouldn't color? They continued telling me that he didn't interact the same way the other kids did, so it would be better for him not to be there.

Better for whom? Certainly for my son, if that was the environment he was in. He was three and a half years old, and the judging had begun!!!

This was supposed to be a Christian preschool, yet because he didn't fit into their perfect little three- and four-year-old mold, he was kicked out. What message was that conveying to our children? How "Christian" was that? And how would I tell my child that he couldn't go back to school because he didn't interact the same way the other kids did?

I had to protect my son from a society that judged and condemned someone who was different—even a small child. How anyone could do that to an innocent child was absolutely beyond my comprehension. Where was compassion and understanding? Where was acceptance and love? Weren't we supposed to be the adults in this world?

Now my search had to expand, not only to seek medical answers but also a safe environment in which my child could be accepted for who he was, not who or what someone said he was supposed to be at three and a half years old.

Disheartened, as Jeffrey was taking a nap, I went to a quiet place and prayed for help and guidance on what to do. I didn't know where to turn, and I knew that it was critical for him to have a positive experience. I prayed that I would be guided, promising that I would listen and trust.

The next morning, as I was taking him to the same park that we had gone to numerous times, I happened to glance over to one side of the road and saw a small Montessori school sign not too far from our neighborhood. Where had that come from? Why hadn't I ever seen that sign as I drove past it almost daily?

A peaceful knowing came into my heart, and I knew without a doubt that that was the school for my son. I asked; I listened; I trusted; and I received.

Of course, I also had to do my part, as I had previously learned a big lesson. I would definitely be more thorough as I paved the way for my son, now and in the future.

I was very honest and upfront with the teachers about what our experience had been and was assured that the Montessori belief had no "mold" for children to fit into. Jeff would not only be free, but encouraged, to be who he was. His uniqueness would be celebrated.

Walking out to my car, I was elated and so grateful. It felt right. And it was.

Jeff expressed an immediate interest in books, and since he was encouraged by his Montessori teachers, he was reading and printing by the age of four. (I still have those books and workbooks.) He was excited about going to school, and when I picked him up each day he was a little chatterbox, laughing and giggling about his day— effervescent sounds to be cherished!

He chattered about his teachers and his friends, and he chattered about the garden he helped plant and the books he read. He loved to read. He read at school; he read in the car; and he read at home, even sneaking out of bed and reading by the night-light in his room.

His teachers were excited about his interests and his progress, and with their continued encouragement, he blossomed into a happy little boy.

We did it! We hit a home run, and, oh, it felt so good!

And we did it our way. My son has never colored. It was a good lesson not to let people put us or our loved ones in boxes.

CHAPTER 10

Jeffrey's few years at the Montessori school were filled with times of rejuvenation as we moved through days of somewhat normal everyday occurrences, each smile and sound of laughter playing in my heart as a full melodic orchestra.

Spending time with my son at the end of a day was special, and I would listen to his excitement about the different things he did at school with his friends and about how nice his teachers were. One such evening, as I was sitting on his bed, he stopped talking and looked beyond me to the right of his room. With a perplexed look on his face, he said, "Mommy, those lights are here. See, Mommy, see?"

I immediately turned my head in the direction he was pointing, and as much as I wanted to acknowledge what he was seeing, I couldn't pretend; I saw nothing, although I didn't question what he was seeing.

"I'm sorry," I said, "but I can't see any lights."

He then looked at me again and pointed. "Mommy, look, there they are. Look, you can see them."

Again I looked, only to still see nothing but the semidarkness in his room. I knew, however, that he was indeed seeing something real to him, and I intuitively knew that these lights weren't scary, but rather, they were there to protect my son. I smiled at him, and I said, "Son, those are your guardian angels. They are watching over you."

Where did those words come from, and why did I say them without any hesitation? I don't know, but after listening to what I had said, he slowly gazed again around his room and then turned to me with a big beautiful smile that lit up my heart. His next words brought joy to my soul, "Mommy, they *are* my angels! Their colors are so pretty."

And that was the end of that conversation, although we have had many similar ones since then. Jeff says, thirty-three years later, that his angels are always with him everywhere he goes—gold, blue, green, pink, and white dots. He sees them, and he says that they bring such comfort knowing that he is never alone.

And thirty-three years later, I still cannot see his angels or mine. Yet I know that they are there, always with us, patiently waiting for us to talk to them and to ask for guidance. They are always waiting to help us, but because we have free will, we must first ask.

What would have happened if I hadn't acknowledged what Jeff was seeing? Would he have been "shut down"? What messages do we give our children when we can't "see" or "hear" what they do? Are we discounting what they are really experiencing? Oh, to be an open child again, full of wonderment—not doubting, but believing; not closed, but open; not judging, but accepting. It is that childlike innocence that we tend to shut down as we try to fit into Earth's society.

CHAPTER 11

Second grade brought a new school. Unfortunately, the Montessori school only went through first grade, so it was time to move out into a new environment. Because of our past experience, however, the unknown was scary, and I approached it with much trepidation. At the same time, I felt that both my son and I had grown from that experience; it had eventually led us to the right place for Jeff's early foundation, and I had learned to become stronger and more assertive when asking necessary questions.

I ultimately found a small private school, and after thoroughly interviewing both the principal and the teacher, I felt confident that we had been led to the right school for my son.

It was a small school, kindergarten through twelfth grade. The second grade had a total of twelve students with one teacher teaching all subjects, affording her the opportunity and time to really work with and get to know each student.

It also had an indoor pool for swimming classes. The dining experience was somewhat unique in that every student in the school ate at the same time along with their teacher. The meals were served family style, creating a warm and inviting atmosphere for all as the young ones interacted with their respective teachers, as well as other teachers and older students.

Jeff flourished in that environment. He was able to learn and experiment with new and exciting things. He continued to love reading his books, and he was encouraged to nurture that love while broadening his interests.

He made friends with his classmates and seemed to be somewhat accepted for who he was—just a little boy like all the others. Yes, he was slower when he ran. Yes, he had difficulties when climbing stairs and playing outdoor games. Yes, he had to sit closer to the front of the room in order to see the blackboard and hear his teacher. But he was still just a little boy who wanted to fit in with his friends.

The school year came to a close and, along with it, came a choice of either skipping third grade, because academically Jeff was so far ahead of the other students, especially in reading and comprehension, or continuing with his friends in third grade while his new teacher worked with him on an accelerated level. Not bad for a child who would never be able to walk, talk, or function on any level!

After much discussion with Jeff and his teachers on the pros and cons, we all decided that he would stay with his friends. What a great decision that was! His wonderful teacher borrowed some sixth grade books, so Jeff was able to be challenged on his individual level while still experiencing the social benefit of being with his friends.

And so it continued through fourth grade, at which time his new teacher suggested that we have Jeff tested to see just how high he was excelling in various subjects so that he could continue to learn at his own level. The tests indicated that his reading comprehension was at a twelfth grade level.

During that time, the school had gotten its first computers (remember, this was over thirty years ago) and had set up a computer science lab. Because Jeffrey had tested so far above his grade level in every subject except math, his teacher designed an entire individual curriculum, including letting him help the computer science teacher with first- through eighth-grade students. What an absolute thrill that was for him, this little boy who had defied all odds of living!

I will forever be grateful to both the Montessori school and Radford School for accepting and encouraging a little boy who walked differently and had physical challenges. They shaped his life both academically and emotionally, as he knew that even though he couldn't run as fast, see as well, or hear as well as his friends, his mind worked beautifully. And with each academic award that he received, those little legs carried him proudly to the stage.

CHAPTER 12

Although Jeffrey was accepted at Radford and was a happy little boy, there were times when he would get teased about the way he walked, especially when he would be on the playground. Some kids were curious and would ask him why he walked the way he did. Even grown people would stare and make comments when we would go out. Jeffrey was becoming more aware of his differences, and he wanted so badly to be like all the other kids.

During those times he would come to me and softly ask, "Why me, Mommy? Why me?"

How sad those conversations were, because I had no answers. I couldn't "fix him," although I would have done anything if I could have.

I felt so helpless. I would hold him and acknowledge his hurtful questions, and then follow up with praise for the great qualities he had and assure him of how much he was loved.

Did I handle his questions correctly? Should I have done anything differently? I don't know. But I do know that I did the best I knew how to do.

During one of our "why me" conversations about his legs, after a particularly hurtful comment from a woman sitting in the next booth at a restaurant, I told Jeff that if and when he ever wanted us to talk with a doctor about the possibility of surgery to help straighten his legs that I would do so. That seemed to make him feel better. I don't know, but perhaps it gave him a little bit of hope that he might be able to feel and look like his friends when they walked, ran, and played.

As much as I absolutely hated the thought of my son going through more physical pain and suffering, I knew that I would do anything I possibly could to support him. He had no choice in the other surgeries and procedures, but he would be the one making the decision on this one. I also understood his deep yearning for normalcy. He just wanted to look and feel like other kids instead of always being different.

The topic never occurred again until one day many months later as we were walking in the woods in the mountains of Arizona. He looked up at me and said, "Mommy, I'm ready."

That's all he said, but I knew what he was telling me. I asked him if he was sure, to which he replied that he just wanted a chance to see if he could walk straight so that people wouldn't stare and make fun of him. He told me that it made him feel so sad when people did that.

A moment of extreme sadness came over me when I heard my little boy's words. He was willing to go through more pain and suffering temporarily so that he could perhaps avoid a lifetime of it.

Thus, the next surgery was scheduled.

When the day arrived, and the nurse was getting him prepped, he looked at her and said in his little high voice, "I'm gonna walk straight, and then people won't make fun of me and hurt me."

She nodded her head while giving him a hug and a bright smile of encouragement, and then she looked up at me with tears glistening in her eyes. My little man had touched another heart.

I kissed Jeffrey and told him yet again that God was with him and his angels were surrounding him, and then I stepped aside and watched as they wheeled him away from me through those now familiar hospital doors. This time, however, he had the most beautiful look on his face, and his smile held such anticipation of hope.

Oh, how I wanted to go with him! How I yearned to hold him and protect him! But again, I woodenly walked to the waiting room, sat down, and waited for what seemed to be endless hours. Not talking, not moving, I was simply waiting while sending white light and healing energy to my precious brave little boy who had such a strong desire to "fit in" so that people wouldn't hurt him. There were no tears this time, just total focus on my child.

The surgery went well according to the doctor, but Jeffrey would be in a lot of pain for a while. Both legs had casts from his ankles to his hips, but I was assured that the hospital staff would keep him as comfortable as possible.

More physical pain, yet he chose to go through that to look normal, to not have to go through such emotional pain of teasing and extremely hurtful words and actions. I still ask myself today what kind of society we have that innocent children have to experience such hurt and heartache. Why can't we accept and love one another regardless of outer looks, recognizing and acknowledging that we all come from the same place? We all have our stories; some just show more than others. We all want love and acceptance. We all have our journey to walk with our own purpose.

I was waiting in Jeffrey's room when he was brought back from surgery. He was still groggy, but as I took his hand in mine, he looked at me with a tiny smile before he closed his eyes and went back to sleep. As I continued sitting next to his bed while holding his hand and constantly talking to him, I experienced emotions from agony to helplessness to hopefulness.

His doctor had told us that Jeff's recovery time would be lengthy. The casts would have to stay on his legs for a minimum of thirty days. He would start physical therapy while he was in the hospital and continue with a physical therapist for three months after the casts were removed.

I watched my son struggle with intense pain when he took his first steps at the parallel bars. He worked so hard, and the hospital staff fell in love with this brave child with the positive attitude and driving force.

For instance, when his doctor came by one time after surgery to check on him and offered Jeff some ice cream, he responded that he would rather have yogurt because that was better for him and would help him heal faster. Needless to say, the doctor smiled and asked the nurse to please get this young man yogurt right away. And yogurt was included on his tray every day until he left the hospital. (He still eats yogurt every day, although he also likes his ice cream).

I remember talking with a mother whose child was in the same room as Jeff, when all of a sudden my son exclaimed, "Mommy, I feel God's hands on my legs. I feel them right here, Mommy," and he pointed to an area of his casts.

The woman and I immediately stopped talking, and as I looked at my special son lying there in his hospital bed, I saw an absolute glow of wonderment on his face, and I silently thanked God again for entrusting me with His little angel on earth. This was yet another lesson from my little "teacher."

How I would love to be able to say that Jeffrey's legs have been straight since that surgery, but sadly, I cannot. We knew there was a chance that the surgery wouldn't be successful permanently, but at least he was able to feel "normal" for a time in his life, and those memories will stay with us forever.

Jeff continued to flourish in school, and now he wanted to learn to ride a bicycle just like his friends. Although he still experienced difficulties with balance, I agreed that it was time for him to feel that freedom and experience yet another accomplishment that the doctors said he would never do. (Would you say we were checking them off?)

The following Christmas, when Jeff was eight years old, Santa brought him a shiny yellow and black Schwinn bicycle. He was so excited when he saw that little bike sitting under the Christmas tree that morning! He just kept saying over and over, "I can do it! I can do it!" His eyes sparkled with excitement, and his huge smile illuminated the room that Christmas morning, and I vowed that he would indeed ride his beloved bicycle, regardless of how long it would take.

Every afternoon and every weekend for months and months, we would ride up and down the cul-de-sac where we lived; Jeff riding his shiny bike with the training wheels, his little sister following on her pretty pink Princess tricycle, and me jogging beside them. We went back and forth and back and forth for hours at a time. They never seemed to get tired, and the loud laughter we shared filled the cul-de-sac.

Then came the Saturday morning when the training wheels were removed. Jeffrey was ready; he walked his bicycle up the driveway to the street, put his feet on the pedals, and took off with me running beside him holding his bike upright while he pedaled. This continued for weeks and weeks every day after school and weekends. I would hold the seat for balance, eventually turning loose for very brief periods while those little legs pushed up and down, up and down until finally one day he took off on his own. How incredibly exciting! He had done it!

As his little sister, Stephanie, and I were running behind him laughing and cheering, she all of a sudden looked up at the sky and exclaimed in her sweet little four-year-old voice, "Look, mommy, the angels are smiling down at Jeffy."

Smiling down, indeed! As parents, we can all recall the joy and excitement as our children rode their first bicycle solo. And here was a child who, medically speaking, would never accomplish that! Faith, determination, strength, trust, angels, and God—perhaps a combination of all working together!

Again, this was a lesson that we could all strive to learn. Don't ever let others, regardless who they are, determine what you believe or don't believe. Don't ever give anyone your power. For you see, a tiny baby chose to live against all odds; an infant chose to learn and to grow; a young boy chose to walk, talk, and ride his bike even though the medical experts said that wasn't possible. My baby would not survive, much less walk, talk, sit up by himself, feed himself, dress himself, ride a bicycle, or drive a car, but I didn't accept those words. I just simply would not accept them!

Yes, I totally understand that there are situations and challenges that people, even innocent children, have to experience for whatever reason. Just as I acknowledge and praise our doctors and nurses who have devoted their lives to helping all of us, and I am so very thankful that they have chosen that path. I'm simply suggesting and urging all of us to open up and look deep within ourselves to the possibilities that are perhaps there. Don't accept the word "no" until you have explored all avenues, and explored them again. So many times those answers, regardless of what they are, come with the understanding and knowledge that we already have within each of us. I strongly encourage you to seek and acknowledge your own inner strength that can perhaps create miracles, just as a young boy did. What a beautiful gift we can give ourselves!

CHAPTER 13

The following years continued with various experiences—some joyful and fun, others resulting in buckets of tears and such wrenching heartache that I would have to escape for a short while to have time alone in order to process.

Jeff continued to soar academically at school, and he felt good about himself even though he still had to endure cruel comments and looks at times wherever he went.

Then, one day, when Jeff was eleven years old, his father accepted a job in California, and after three years, Jeff had to leave the school he loved.

We left shortly after school was out, so I would have the summer to research new schools. We arrived in California amidst both trepidation and excitement, as we knew that familiarity would become a thing of the past and yet new paths would materialize. Of course, the kids, being eleven and eight years old, were very excited about living near Disneyland and the ocean and beaches, and we had a great time that summer. We played and played and took advantage of all the fun things to do.

I found a small school for Jeff and Steph, and we settled down in our new environment, enjoying our lives in California, not knowing what lay ahead.

Two years later, our world, as we knew it, spun out of control. Our family unit that had existed for almost sixteen years imploded.

By the time Jeff was in his first year of middle school, he could sense the change in the dynamics of his secure, or so he thought at the time, home life. Ultimately, his father left.

Jeff began to act out, demonstrating bouts of intense anger, shouting words and running away, only to go a short distance and then come back apologizing and sobbing.

This quiet, serene child had become enraged as he helplessly watched the world he had known, the only safe place, literally crumble. He watched as I, his 100 percent security, struggled while desperately trying to hold everything together.

I should have known that he could see through my false bravery, but oh, how I tried to hide my absolutely crippling fear as I grappled with how I would be able to financially take care of my children. How was I going to be able to afford the many doctors' appointments that were vital for my son's life? How could I possibly fail him after he had fought so very hard to come through such pain and dark times? How could I afford to be away from my children when one parent had already completely deserted them, and how could I financially afford not to be away?

The unbelievable agony and extreme soul-wrenching fear was almost too much to bear, and I struggled to barely get through the days. My inner strength that had carried me through so many extremely challenging experiences seemed to dwindle, and I ultimately sank into a deep depression.

The overwhelming fear of not being able to provide for my children sapped my energy and my power. I could no longer pretend.

I could no longer carry on. I could no longer be. My mind was so tired, my heart so empty, and my body so weak that I had no more fight left. An engulfing veil of bleakness enveloped my entire being, and I slowly slipped into a place of blissful nothingness: no thoughts, no worries, no strength—simply nothing.

Was it a long overdue much-needed rest? Was it gentle loving protection from my soul and the angels? Was it my inner strength revamping for what lay ahead? Or could it possibly be all of the above?

I lay in bed for almost a week, and to this day, those days and nights remain a blur. I don't question it. I don't judge it. It just is what happened.

Finally, words seemingly sounding from afar pushed through the encompassing dark veil.

"Linda, what will happen to Jeff and Steph if you leave this earth? Please think about that!" These desperate words were spoken from my beloved sister who is now a beautiful loving angel still watching over and protecting my children and me.

Just one question with few words that raced through my being, reaching deep, deep down to the depths of my despair and sparking the tip of awareness and hope that had lain dormant within. As I began my journey back to "life," soaring upward through that tunnel, I immediately experienced an abundance of love, compassion, energy, and strength.

I was, once again, ready for what lay ahead. I truly believe my extreme fear coupled with the overwhelming fear that I had stored within my body over the years totally sapped my entire strength, allowing me to be gently held for a period of nurturing rest, perhaps preparing me for what was to come.

Now it was time to plunge forward, again fighting for my children by going deep within to pull up the strength and energy I needed, not realizing what incredibly dark and confusing times lay ahead.

During that time, while continuing to deal with my own crazy, out-of-control world filled with doubts and fears as to how I could possibly go on, I would not allow myself to sink back into the level of deep wrenching despair from which I had emerged. I had no choice but to dig down to pull from my reserve strength. I had to shore up my kids so that they would, hopefully, feel that although their foundation of security had indeed been badly shaken, it had not been destroyed.

I still had no idea how I would be able to support them, but I knew that somehow I would. Many times, I felt like a hamster or a gerbil on a wheel, going round and round and round, with more stuff thrown on, causing the wheel to spin faster and faster and get heavier and heavier.

Ultimately, a ray of sunshine pushed through the dense clouds in the form of two very dear friends, one being Tom, the man who had gently held me up when my son had been born and throughout various subsequent challenges, and the other being Irma, his wife, a very special friend with whom I had shared so many talks during both sad and happy times.

My children and I stayed with them for almost a month during that crazy upheaval in our lives. Then it was time to go back to reality and deal with whatever I needed to so that we could move forward.

A couple of days before our departure, my friends said that they wanted to talk with me. We had discussed how Jeff was acting out, and they were very concerned. They said that they felt Jeff desperately needed a dad right then, and Tom wanted to be that dad figure for him. They suggested that Jeff stay with them for the school year and go back to the school that he had loved so that I could focus on what needed to be done with the other part of my unraveling life. Of course, if I agreed, the final decision would be up to Jeff.

My initial reaction was no way could I leave him, yet I realized that that was my fear and insecurity talking. If I truly wanted what was best for my son and my daughter, I would accept their generous, loving offer. After all three of us discussed their suggestion with Jeffrey, the decision was made. Irma told him that she knew he would miss me, but things would get better.

Jeff looked at her and said," No. You see, I know my mom loves me and always will, but I need a dad right now." And so for one school year my son went back to the security of the school that was familiar under the loving and fun guidance of two dear friends, to whom I will be forever grateful.

It was nine long months away from my son, but at least I was able to talk with him every day and see him every three or four weeks when I would fly him out to visit. I was excited to see him each time and elated when he would get off the plane full of laughter and excitement. Although I dreaded Sunday afternoons when it would be time to put him back on the plane, I knew that it was the right thing to do, and it was the best gift I could give him at that time.

Meanwhile, I had the opportunity to focus on my precious daughter as well as on the craziness of the time. I had to pretend to only one child that all was right—or at least as right as I could make it. We had silly pajama parties, with the two of us dancing around the room. They were our special fun times together, and I cherished those day-to-day memories with my little girl, knowing that someday we would all three once again be together.

CHAPTER 14

And then there were four again. A man came into my life at a time when I most definitely wasn't looking. Not only was I not looking, but I was absolutely against any type of relationship other than as a friend.

I was 100 percent focused on dealing with the all-encompassing, negative mire surrounding my children and me, that ever-present sucking quicksand that threatened to take me down once again. But this time I knew that I could not and would not succumb to that false sense of power constantly eating away at my emotional being.

I had taken that enormous step to reclaim my power, and I would keep it, finally realizing that the only way someone else could have it was if I gave it away; it was mine, and only mine, to give. I was fighting for my two children as well as my own survival, and I would fight mightily. I was the mighty mama bear protecting her cubs!

Mighty, yes, yet at the same time it felt so good to have someone around to talk with and laugh with, as the sound of genuine laughter had become so foreign to me. Now it was like a waterfall gently cascading its pure, refreshing water into a peaceful, mirror-like stream, replenishing my energy.

It was time for Jeff to visit again. I had told him about my new friend, and he was excited about meeting him. On the way home from the airport, he looked at me with a worried look on his face and asked me if I thought my friend would like him. "Yes, Son," I replied. "He has heard all about you and is looking forward to spending some time with all of us." Then he seemed to relax, although I could tell that he was still concerned about being accepted.

The next morning, as Jeffrey was getting his bike out of the garage, Ken, my new friend, met him. They talked for a few minutes, and later, Ken told me that the words "That's my son" had appeared crystal clear in his mind.

Where did those words come from? Was there something bigger that we were unaware of? Was that our next path on this journey we call life?

All four of us spent a fun-filled weekend together with lots of laughter. I was amazed to see Jeff's excitement as he and Ken continued talking and hanging out together. At one point, he ran into the house to tell me that the chain on his bike had broken and Ken was taking him to the bike shop to get another one so that he could fix it. It was such a simple gesture, but to Jeff, it was monumental that a male other than his uncles or Tom would want to spend time with him.

Then it was time to take him back to the airport. Although I knew that temporarily being with Tom and Irma was the best thing for my son, I dreaded those Sunday afternoons, knowing that it would be another three weeks before I would see him again.

As we were all waiting for his plane to arrive, Jeff looked at Ken and said, "Would you mind if I call you Dad?"

Ken replied immediately, "I would love that, Son." And so it was.

How often do we resist instead of simply letting go and trusting? How often do our fears paralyze us—fear of doing the wrong thing, fear of making a wrong decision, fear of making a mistake, or fear of what others will think? Fear (an acronym for "false expectations appearing real") is just one of many emotions, yet it can become enormous and overbearing in our lives if we allow it to. Let go and let God—such a simple concept, yet it is so difficult for many of us. Yes, we pray to God—then we tell Him how and when "it" needs to be done. He must have a great sense of humor as He listens to His children try to take control of all things!

The end of the school year arrived, and it was time for Jeff to come back home. Although he loved his time with Tom and Irma and going back to Radford for a year, he was excited about my upcoming wedding and excited about having a new dad. As my son took his rightful place in our soon-to-be new family, the sun blessed us with its warming rays, and the stars sparkled brightly upon our extended family unit.

CHAPTER 15

Bullying! This is a word that we have heard and seen so often in the media in the past years. We have seen and heard heartbreaking incidents happening to our kids of all ages. Some of these incidents have been so horrific that our beautiful young people are taking their own lives.

Entering high school after returning to California was an exciting time for Jeff. He would be able to continue to learn so that he could prepare for college, for which he had such high aspirations. Amidst this excitement, we enrolled him in a private religious school with a great reputation, thinking that would be a safe, highly academic environment where he could thrive.

Jeff absolutely loved learning new things. Human anatomy, electronics, history, outer space, the solar system, the universe, the history of our planet, current events—he loved them all, and we used to say that he was like a big sponge just soaking up all the knowledge that he could possibly attain. He was so proud of his mind because he knew that was a part of him where he could excel. Even though some visible parts of his body were "inferior" according to him and others, he had a magnificent mind that allowed him to shine and to be proud.

After a while, however, we began seeing changes in our son that concerned us. For instance, the school hadn't ordered enough books, so they would open a small bookstand across the large campus for a brief time when the books came in, and the students were expected to run and stand in line for their missing books. Meanwhile, they were expected to do their required work, totally setting up a path of failure. How could students possibly complete their homework if they didn't have their books? It just didn't make sense, and for someone like Jeff, who was always academically at the top of his class, this was devastating.

Each day, he would run as fast as he could across campus to get his books, but because he was slower than the other kids, he never could make it to the front of the line before they closed. We tried to let Jeff work out this problem on his own, but after more than a week of this absurd policy my husband, Jeff's new dad, offered to go with him to the bookstand, thinking that surely if they saw a parent with their child, the ridiculous problem would be resolved. Unfortunately, however, that was not the case, and the two of them stood in line together for three days before Jeff had all of his books.

As a student, Jeff simply wanted to learn, and instead, we later learned from others, he was spit on in history class, the spit rolling from the top of his head down his face. The odometer on his beloved bicycle was destroyed (he had a goal of riding it one thousand miles, and he was within a few miles of being able to complete that sense of accomplishment). He was totally surrounded by a circle of bullies while others looked on and cheered. To this day, we still don't know what happened, as that devastating experience continues to be deeply buried. He was taunted and ridiculed so badly that one day he simply retreated to a place of escape.

Ken and I were in the car, when all of a sudden, I had this horrible feeling that something was terribly wrong with Jeff and that we had to immediately get to him. So without questioning me, Ken turned the car around, driving as fast as possible to get to the school.

As we went running into the school office, I was told that my son was with the principal, and we were hurriedly escorted to her office. I immediately saw Jeff; he was sitting in a chair, just staring into space, with three women standing around him looking as if they didn't know what to do. One look and I knew that he had gone to a place where no one could touch him or hurt him. He had gone to his own safe cocoon. I looked at the three women just standing there. I wanted to scream, "Leave him alone! Was it too much to ask that someone pick up a phone and call me, his mother? Can't you see what has happened?"

As I led my broken child away, my heart was aching for the tiny newborn who had fought so very hard to survive, for the child who had asked, "Why me, Mommy?"—the young boy who simply couldn't take the horrific cruelty any longer.

Thus began another time of frantically searching for answers. How could we reach that place where our son had retreated? Who could we trust to help us? We were fighting an invisible unknown, not knowing where to turn.

This was something we couldn't see or touch, and it was frightening. We immediately took him to a psychiatrist, who quickly put him on pills, which just made him zombie-like. We questioned the doctor, but he assured us that we were doing the right thing. We didn't know where else to turn, and we felt totally helpless as we saw our son slipping away.

We then went to other doctors, the result being more medication. Something was wrong, but doctors were supposed to know what to do, weren't they? Could we trust them, or should we not trust them? We were afraid to give Jeff the pills, and we were afraid not to give him the pills.

The days turned into nights over and over as we tried to get through this thick shell that had completely enveloped our son. He no longer knew how to button his shirt. He couldn't remember how to brush his teeth or wash his face. He couldn't make a decision on what to eat. He couldn't express any wants or needs. He couldn't make *any* decision.

We would take him to G-rated movies, hoping that he could comprehend something, but he would leave confused. We would slowly explain these simple movies, but it was to no avail. He simply could not comprehend, and nothing we tried could reach him.

He was such a gentle soul, like a robot with an ever-so-sweet smile. I remember Ken and me tucking him into bed each night after brushing his teeth for him. As we both hugged him, he would look into our eyes and softly mutter, "Please don't leave me. Please be here when I wake up."

What had I done to my son? How could I have failed him and been so completely wrong? Why didn't I know better? Was there something I should have known? How could I have put my son in such a school? These are all questions I would constantly ask as I would lie awake night after night, berating myself. Yet somewhere, deep down, a little voice would gently push through all this self-doubt, assuring me that I had done the best I could possibly do. I was encouraged not to spend time on the "whys" and the "hows" but to move forward with strength and conviction to follow my inner voice.

We never left Jeffrey during his time of darkness. We were fortunate that he could go to work with us each day, and he did. He was so gentle and innocent, and our coworkers immediately provided him a safety net. They never pushed; they never asked questions; they simply accepted.

One lady, in particular, who had been at the office for a short time, reached out to Jeff with such accepting, gentle, loving arms that he slowly began to respond to her, and after a while, she asked if Jeff could go home with her for an hour. He softly responded that he would like that; it was the first time during those long months that he had expressed any interest in anything.

A long, very loving relationship began that day, and many years later, Janice and Gordon are still in Jeff's life. He truly loves them like parents and even refers to them as his second mom and dad.

We have all heard of Earth angels. I totally believe that Janice and Gordon are Jeffrey's Earth angels. I also know that Joyce and Ray, my sister and brother-in-law, were Jeff's Earth angels at one time before they crossed over to become his guardian angels.

Jeffrey slowly started coming back to us, each small accomplishment bringing joy into our hearts. When he asked for a particular food to eat, I became so excited; I would have gone anywhere to get it. The first time he walked into the kitchen fully dressed, I wanted to dance around the room—actually, I did!

Our prayers had been answered. Our son had come back to us.

More than twenty years later, we still do not know everything that happened to Jeff, but we do know that he lost two years of his life because of bullying. We do know that his life was forever changed because of horrible cruelty that occurred in a supposedly safe environment with supposedly safe administrators with whom we had entrusted our son. We do know that he continues, to this day, to live with tremendous fear and emotional pain from the severe cruelty that pierced his soul so long ago.

How utterly sad it is that cruelty is allowed in our schools, on our playgrounds, on school campuses, in restaurants, at the movies, and in stores; it sometimes happens in places we would least expect, but it still does happen. My son experienced it all. His totally safe place had been at home with family and special friends who were "adopted" family, but just think of all the kids who don't have that safety net.

One beautiful sunny day, when we were sitting in our backyard talking, I asked Jeff what had happened at school that particular day to cause him such tremendous hurt. He just looked me in the eyes and replied, "Mom, I was emotionally raped."

That's all he said, and I instinctively knew not to press. Whatever he had experienced was deeply locked up. The best I could do for him was to continue providing professional help with a doctor he liked and trusted—and to just shower him with unconditional love.

CHAPTER 16

It was now time to find another school. Although my desire was to keep him with us at all times where he would be safe, I knew that I couldn't do that. Again, that was about my fears. We had to show our son that we fully believed in him and that we had confidence in his abilities. It was crucial for him to believe in his own strength. So we enrolled him in a small private school where, if he could make up the work for all the months he had missed, he would be able to progress to the next grade. Although they expressed their doubts to us, to their amazement, his mind, indeed, did return with a vengeance, thirsting for the knowledge he had missed. And even though we knew that wasn't a long-term school for him because of limited academics, it filled an important gap that gave him the opportunity to move forward.

He experienced bullying at this school, too, but this time Ken and I were more aware of what signs to look for, and we addressed our concerns immediately with the school staff. We had shared with them what our son had been through, and they assured us that they would be on alert in the classrooms and on the school grounds. We also encouraged Jeff to talk with us each evening so that we could have open discussions about what he had experienced and how he was feeling. Some of those discussions were disturbing, but he always told us how much better he felt afterwards.

We wanted our talks to be fun and uplifting so that we could end with positive energy. Sometimes they were short and sometimes they were quite lengthy. Either way, he knew that that was his special time, and when he would go to bed with a smile on his face, we had smiles on ours too.

As I stated earlier, I wanted to keep Jeffrey in the safe cocoon of his family and friends, but I knew that he had to step out to experience life. I knew that he had to be given the opportunity to step out in confidence to achieve his aspirations of going to college, to believe in himself, and to never give up.

We had thought we had made the right decision when we enrolled him in a supposedly superior religious high school the first time, but our son had lost many, many months of his life—months he could never get back. Furthermore, the extreme bullying and cruelty continued to have an ongoing negative impact on Jeff's life in so many ways.

He had already attended two high schools, and we were at a loss where to go next, being fearful of making a wrong choice. However, after Ken, Jeff, and I eliminated the remaining schools in our area, we all decided to check out a public high school in a different school district. All of us felt positive after talking with the principal and some of the teachers about his previous experiences, so it was decided that he would be enrolled and that we would move into a nearby neighborhood so that this could be accomplished.

Jeff was really excited about his new school and continued to make great strides in his studies. His mind, once again, was like a sponge, soaking up knowledge, and he would come home from school each day full of excitement.

During this time, a gym teacher took a special interest in him. He, of course, was aware that Jeff couldn't do many of the activities that other students did effortlessly, but he noticed that when Jeff was on the track, he hardly ever tired. He wasn't anywhere near the fastest, nor could he participate in relays. He didn't have a smooth stride, but oh, how he loved to run around that track.

That school track became gym class for Jeff, and the first time he brought home his report card with an A in PE, his eyes were dancing, and the pure joy on his face was magical. He had accomplished something physically! Forget the fact that he had made As in all of his academic classes. That was normal. But something physical? Now *that* was a huge accomplishment for a boy who couldn't walk "normally," for a boy who had been maliciously ridiculed for looking "different."

What an absolute joy those days were—even if only for a short while.

Chapter 17

One afternoon, a call turned our lives upside down yet again. The school secretary's voice was intense as she said, "You need to come to school as soon as possible. Something is wrong with your son!"

They were incomprehensible words. As I threw down the phone and ran to my car, I was praying out loud: "Please, God, not again! Please, not again!"

Upon screeching into the school parking lot, I ran as fast as I possibly could to get to Jeff. I saw him sitting in a chair. I quickly went to him, but he seemed to be looking right through me as he rapidly rattled off numerous numbers and equations.

And then he ran! What was happening? What had caused this bizarre behavior, and who or what was he running from?

"Oh, God, please help him! Please give me the words to get through to him!" I cried as I ran after my son. "Please give me the strength to help him!"

I became aware of others running too. After a while, Jeff stopped and just looked at us like a confused, wounded animal.

I then heard the familiar voice of my husband telling everyone to get back, that his mother was the only one who would be able to approach him. I cautiously and slowly stepped toward Jeff, speaking soft, loving words; his eyes slowly turned from panic to trust. As I got close enough, I reached out and gently took him into my arms and just held him, again giving him what strength I had. It was all for him, this lost soul.

What had happened to cause that overwhelming fear and break from reality? We simply don't know.

Again, my son went to another place and time where we couldn't go. What devastating sorrow it is to know that your child has gone to an unknown place. Each morning, I woke up with a guarded hope that he would somehow find his way back; each day, I looked for the slightest sign that he had returned to us; each night, I prayed that the next day would be "the day."

Why couldn't I reach him? Why did this have to happen again? Hadn't he been through enough? *God, where are you? Why can't you make him well? Why can't you bring him back?*

I slowly made my way through the thick fog, blindly reaching out with each step I took to grab hold of this young, lost boy, to enfold him in my arms; I promised again that I would always be with him.

"Take my strength," I cried. "I will carry you. Just please come back!"

We continued on the seesaw of life through the following days and nights: a piercing cry coming from deep within, an overwhelming yearning erupting from my soul, and a frantic look for even a tiny sign that my son was again emerging from that unknown place.

And then, one day, Jeff looked at me, and I saw a tiny smile tentatively emerging into a more definite one. He had come back yet again! Joyful tears flowed from my eyes as I held him in my arms.

I no longer try to understand it. I don't even know if it is mine to understand. I simply celebrate.

CHAPTER 18

Laughter and fun interspersed with the usual stuff of life as we all continued our journey. By this time, Jeffrey was in college, and even though he rarely participated in any type of social life, he loved the academics, and he loved his professors, with whom he felt accepted.

Eating alone, however, facing the wall at the very back of the cafeteria was a normal routine in our son's world, as was consuming his food as quickly as possible so that he could hurriedly exit a room filled with potential terror—or so he thought. An overwhelming fear of a group of cruel people making fun of him, ridiculing the way he walked, and verbalizing hurtful words had become part of Jeff's life.

At the same time, he was so proud of being able to accomplish his goal of attending college after all of his challenging experiences in high school. He was also really proud of his highly functioning mind and his resulting grades.

The independence he experienced of living on his own three states away from family was exciting for him, although he was close enough to be able to drive to his special aunt and uncle's home on weekends. He really looked forward to the long drive by himself when he would come home during holidays. He loved being home, and he loved the trip back to school too.

He was feeling good about himself in spite of his fears, and he was excited about his upcoming graduation.

He almost made it—and then we received that by this time familiar dreaded call, the one that instantly seared through layers of skin and muscle, piercing right through the heart.

I hardly heard the conversation as I hung up the phone and slumped against the wall.

"I can't! I won't let this happen again!" I cried. I knew how extremely important that college degree was to our son: a symbol that he had made it in spite of all his hardships; a symbol that his mind was okay; a symbol that he had proven the doctors wrong when they said so long ago that he would never walk or talk or function on his own. His mind was so important to him, for he had such challenges with other parts of his physical body. His mind gave him strength and hope.

I heard it in his voice—the fear, the "slipping away." He was so close to fulfilling his dream of that college diploma; there was only a month to go. I had to get to him, and I had to help him through that descending fog that threatened to once again envelop him. Oh no, this wouldn't happen again. I would fight until there was no fight left.

For the next month, I stayed with Jeffrey. I took him to school, assuring him that I would wait in the car while he attended his classes so that he could see me the minute he left his classroom, knowing that he would be safe.

We ate together; we studied together, repeating the same information over and over. I fought for my son with every source of energy I could muster. We could do this together. There simply was no other option. I knew we had to, and I gently worked and worked with him. He could not feel defeated on this oh-so-important dream!

As we would both lie down for a much-needed night's rest, I would pray so very hard for the strength to get through the next day. I prayed for the right words to get through to him. I prayed for the right actions to help him stay with us. I prayed for guidance and faith.

The first day of finals arrived, and Jeff stepped out of the car, this brave young man walking to his classroom, glancing back for reassurance that I was still there. Tears began to flow as I prayed and asked his angels to be with him.

Please let him pass! This is so much more than a college diploma. This is a symbol for years and years of tremendous struggle. This is success against all odds. This is an acceptance of himself!

Each day we repeated the same routine, until finally the last exam was over. I knew that I was as nervous as Jeff was while we waited for his grades to be posted. I tried to keep him occupied, but I knew that both of our minds were on those grades.

And then the time came. He did it! He really did it! What exulting joy to see the slow tentative smile turn into a full-fledged giant grin as he turned to me. He had fought hard, and he had come out victorious. How brave he was not to give up.

The day of graduation finally arrived, and as our son walked across that stage and was handed his diploma, he turned to look at his family and friends with the most magnificent, electrifying smile. We all whooped and hollered at the magical moment.

CHAPTER 19

We have heard and seen on the news about doctors prescribing a wrong medication, thus causing tremendous harm to a patient. And so it was with our son.

After graduation Jeff was doing much better, and he was looking forward to staying in California for a short while before driving back home. While he was there, he wanted to see his doctor one more time to thank him for his help.

Although we didn't know it at the time, that visit was the beginning of another roller-coaster ride, taking a tremendously sharp dip into yet another realm.

His doctor was pleased with Jeff's progress and really excited about a new drug that he felt would be superior to the one Jeff was currently taking. The doctor had previously helped Jeff very much, and all of us totally trusted him, so Jeff didn't even think to question his recommendation. In reality, his trusted doctor prescribed a medication that ultimately sent him into a tailspin.

We talked with Jeffrey almost daily, and he would tell us about how much fun he was having. After the first week, however, I felt like something wasn't quite right when we would talk; yet I couldn't figure out what it was. There was just a feeling inside that kept gnawing at me, and over the previous years I had learned to pay attention to my intuition.

The feeling persisted, and when Jeff started talking really fast during some of our conversations, I became even more concerned.

He was driving home in less than a week and was really excited about the trip. I asked if he would like some company. I could fly out and drive back with him. He thanked me, but said that he wanted to do this on his own and would see us the following Saturday.

I respected his wishes, but I became even more apprehensive as the days passed and our conversations continued.

The day before he left, I asked again if I could fly out and drive back with him. I said that I was ready for a road trip, but I think he saw right through me and told me not to worry. He said he would see me in two days.

Time seemed to drag as I waited for him to call, not knowing where he was, but when he did call on that first night, by the end of our conversation, I absolutely knew that something was wrong. I just didn't know what.

I asked if he was feeling okay and he said yes, and that he was really enjoying the trip. I again asked if he would like for me to ride with him the rest of the way, but he replied that he wanted to complete the trip on his own.

When he arrived, I knew immediately that something was wrong. He was talking very fast and couldn't sit down for long. Ken and I would talk with him and ask him questions, but his answers didn't make sense.

Jeff was up wandering around the house most of the night. He would try to lie down and then he would immediately get up again. This behavior continued all night, the next day, and the next night. He said that he just wasn't tired, but we knew that it was so much more than that. We just didn't know what. This was unlike anything we had dealt with before.

What was happening to our son? As much as we tried, we simply could not get through to him. He was making no sense whatsoever when he talked.

We were on a fast train speeding into yet another unknown, but this was a completely new experience.

How were we to handle this? What could we say or do to penetrate this out-of-control train threatening our son? I felt I had grabbed on to the caboose, and we were careening around dangerously sharp curves at a speed faster than I had ever experienced; I simply hung on.

I frantically called Jeff's doctor in California for help; the one we had totally trusted and who had helped him before when he was so sick. I explained what was happening, but all he said was that he didn't know what to do.

By this time Jeff also realized that something was wrong with him and was really scared. And after seeing a local doctor who just wanted to prescribe more pills, Jeff personally called his "trusted" California doctor to ask for help. However, this doctor wouldn't even take the time to take Jeff's calls. This terrified young man, who had been his patient for years, desperately reached out to the doctor but to no avail. There were no responses to our pleas for help.

The whole world, our world, was spinning out of control. As we desperately tried to stay ahead of Jeff to anticipate his next move, I knew that we were losing this overwhelming gigantic battle. Just as the mist slips through one's fingers, so did our son.

We had conquered many battles, somewhat battered, many times slowly limping to the finish line, yet in the end, we had been victorious. Would we be up for yet another battle against another unknown, with nothing to hold on to, nowhere to turn, and no one to turn to?

If we could just understand it, then we could somehow deal with it, whatever "it" was, never realizing that the unknown enemy was just a tiny pill that Jeff was trustingly taking—one tiny pill that was causing such devastating havoc in our son's life.

It seems so clear now, but when we were in the middle of this spiraling world, clarity didn't exist, or at least it didn't for me. As we spun around and around, increasingly faster down this dark hole, I vowed that my son would not travel that dark path alone.

Days turned into sleepless nights as we continued this tremendous struggle, not knowing where to turn. By this time we were all totally exhausted and felt that our only answer was to admit Jeffrey into the hospital for testing. We simply had to find out what was wrong.

Finally, we saw a tiny glimpse of hope. A young doctor walked into the hospital room saying that he wanted to do some tests because he thought that Jeff was on the wrong medication.

Oh my God, could that be? Could it be that simple? And then it hit me like a ton of bricks! It was shortly after the original doctor had changed Jeff's medication that he started exhibiting this bizarre behavior!

Why hadn't I seen it? Why couldn't I have figured that out? This is a question I have asked myself many times over the years. It seems so clear now, but when we were in the midst of such terrifying turmoil, clarity just didn't exist.

I have heard it said that there are no mistakes in life, simply experiences from which we grow. Well, grow we did! And what is really interesting is that the young doctor who ultimately helped Jeff came into his life and then moved on fairly quickly. I believe that people come into our lives for a reason. Some stay a long time, while others move on after a short while—all making a profound difference. We don't know where the doctor is or if he is still practicing medicine, but we will always be grateful to him for helping us to get back on the right path.

I learned another valuable lesson from that experience. I realized that doctors are human beings like the rest of us. We should be so thankful to them for their desire to help people; they do the best they can with the knowledge they have, but we also need to take the responsibility of being proactive, especially when medication is prescribed. We need to insist on the needed time to ask questions, and if we don't understand the answers the first time, we should ask again and again until we do understand. We need to know what we are putting into our bodies and why.

Was there malice toward Jeffrey? No, I truly believe that the doctor in California just made a horrible mistake, and instead of trying to correct that mistake, he simply ignored it. As Jeff later said, "Mom, he made a bad mistake that time, but I can't forget the good he did for me, too."

Jeff is a forgiving soul. And as we learned that the wrong medication had indeed caused such tremendous havoc in his life, I looked into the eyes of my oh-so-tired son and saw yet again a tiny glimmer of hope.

We had crawled out of the deep black hole once again. And as we watched our son close his eyes and drift into a peaceful sleep, I thanked God and the angels for their guidance and for sending us that special young doctor.

Could these threatening thunderstorms finally begin to recede? Dare we even begin to hope that there would be calm seas in our future? Yet hope is eternal, and faith is an internal foundation on which we stand. Yes, indeed, we will continue to celebrate life!

CHAPTER 20

Years passed with the typical ups and downs of life as Jeffrey continued to deal with challenges. However, he seemed to have more strength to carry him through the rough patches.

We cautiously began to walk on a new path, step by step, and we encountered beautiful, warm rays of sunshine bursting through the clouds at times. Soft, lush green grass began to gently sway in the cool breeze, and from time to time, beautifully colored flowers would open their petals, inviting us to open our hearts, if just a tiny crack, to view the true beauty of life.

We began to see colorful birds singing their soothing melodies, clouds becoming fluffy and lighter, and beautiful butterflies emerging from their tiny cocoons and flying freely for the first time. We took deep, cleansing breaths, inhaling as much of the surrounding beauty as possible, cherishing every moment.

We were truly experiencing this gift of life that God has bestowed upon each of His children—so thankful for the strength and love that continued to blossom, so very thankful for some peace and rest.

Jeff and I had experienced and endured so much of this life together, incurring bloody battle bruises as well as exulting triumphs.

I yearned to continue to envelope him with a loving net of strength, holding my son closely, protecting him from more hurtful occasions, and celebrating our positive times together. But I knew that the time had come for me to gently step aside, encouraging and supporting Jeff to continue on his own journey, for indeed it was his to walk. I would give him words of encouragement, understanding, and love. I would be with him when, and if, he needed me to listen and to gently pick him up. But now it was his time to live his own destiny, to walk his own path, to live his own purpose.

As he set off on his journey almost one thousand miles away to his dream and the place where he felt was home, I again prayed to God that He would send His angels to protect my son and to help me know the right words of encouragement to send him on his way. I prayed for the strength to smile as he drove off to a new territory and a new beginning.

Now I had to be strong for my son from a distance as he cried out to me about his many cruel encounters. Although I wanted to rush to his side, protecting him yet again from life's harsh realities that continued to be a part of his world, I knew that I couldn't. I just listened, validated his hurt and sadness, and always turned the conversation to something positive, even if it was but a tiny nugget. Sometimes our conversations were quite lengthy, and that was okay. In the end, we had to surround ourselves with positive energy.

I flew out to visit as often as I could. We talked for hours and hours. Sometimes we cried; sometimes we laughed; and sometimes he just needed me to listen. Although it was difficult to leave him each time, I knew this was right for him. Time passed, and I could hear his voice get stronger as more and more laughter became a part of our conversations. What a beautiful vibration laughter is! It lights up the world. It can instantly turn dreary gray clouds to beautiful blue skies. It is like a smiling, bright sun shining down to tickle the soul. Laughter is a sound to cherish at all times, especially when it has been so long in coming.

CHAPTER 21

November 2011 was an awe-inspiring month! Jeff was very excited about a four-day spiritual conference he had signed up for and asked me if I would like to join him. We had attended other short spiritual events together, and I would marvel at his self-confidence and excitement during and after each one. He would comment about the safe environment where people didn't seem to judge him, and he felt good about himself. I was very excited to be able to share this magical time with him.

Those four days turned out to be a turning point in Jeff's life, as well as mine. I observed him actually initiating conversations with various people, which is something I had not seen previously, and a bursting happiness filled my soul. That was the first time I had seen a luminous light shine through this grown child of mine, illuminating his spirit while reaching out to touch his spiritual kindred souls. His eyes shone with an enveloping love, and his radiant smile brightened the room; he had discovered a place of unconditional love and acceptance.

Jeff had found his home away from home, where people didn't judge how a person looked on the outside. He had finally found his safe haven where he was totally accepted for who he was, spirit touching spirit. He had found a place where he could simply relax and just be.

What exalting joy filled my soul as I realized that this young man who had fought so hard for survival was now reaping the rewards of his journey.

A beautiful butterfly slowly emerged from a dark, cramped cocoon, again cautiously testing its wings while fluttering in the breeze. And as each speaker shared his or her amazing story and journey, my son's wings seemed to get stronger and stronger. He had lived in that fearful cocoon for so long, but now he was free to truly experience life and love, if only for short intervals.

He was in awe that people wanted to talk with him and actually listen to what he had to say. During lunch breaks, he would even sit down at a table with people already sitting there, which was so different from the young college student who had always sat alone at the back table facing the wall. And at the end of each day, he could hardly wait to talk to me about the new friends he had met and the email addresses they had given him.

This was the beginning of Jeff discovering his own journey of enlightenment and finding his own strength. This was a time when a thread of self-acceptance began to emerge slowly and gently. This was a time when he began to tentatively experience the beautiful value of life on this earthly plane.

Yes, he still has to live in this judgmental world where he continues to be ridiculed and hurt. He still has to endure cruelty and heartache, but now he has found his strong foundation, a beautiful spiritual place where the angels are applauding and surrounding him and his kindred spirits. Each one of us walks our own path toward our unique purpose.

I have seen my son emerge from an almost paralyzing frightened boy into a young man who, even though he still experiences times of fear and heartache, embraces the goodness of others. One of Jeff's greatest joys is when people tell him how much he has helped them just by listening or sharing in his quiet, gentle manner.

I strongly encourage anyone who is currently on a rocky path to never give up—just never give up! Take one day at a time, sometimes one hour or even one minute. Know and believe that sunshine is right behind the ominous dark clouds, just waiting to push through with its beautiful, warm rays.

Fear can be crippling, as it was with my son, but don't be afraid to reach out and hold on to someone, as there is always, always help. We all have our stories, some seemingly more profound than others, but we can push through the darkness, step by step, knowing that we are never alone. We have chosen our journeys, for whatever reason. We might not understand it now, and we may never understand it in this lifetime, but it is ours to walk and experience.

I have always told my children that I believe we have two choices in life: when the ominous dark shadows surround us, we can either stay stuck in the darkness or we can pick ourselves up by the seat of our pants and choose to go forward toward the light.

Sometimes it isn't easy. In fact, at times it can be absolutely daunting, but know that just as my son and I travelled our own turbulent paths, never giving up, so can you!

Does he still see his angels, those iridescent dancing dots? Every day. Everywhere. He is never alone.

PART 2

THE INTERVIEW

December 2011

Jeff's desire is that this book will help ease the way for other people who have physical and/or mental challenges, especially when those challenges have resulted in bullying. Such hurtful acts are oftentimes devastating, at times even ending in death either by the perpetrators or the victims. Jeff shared that there were times when he felt it would have been much easier if he had just left this earth and gone on to a loving place where there was no hurt or heartache, where unconditional love was abundant. Actually, a few times he came close to ending his life, filled with devastating thoughts that he was a mistake, that he just couldn't endure any more pain and suffering. But there was a tiny seed buried deep inside that assured him that God doesn't make mistakes and that he had a purpose to fulfill. He also feels very strongly that his angels have protected him through dark times with their powerful unconditional love, and they have given him the strength and guidance to continue his journey.

The words that follow are from a conversation that Jeff and I had in December 2011. He wanted to personally share some of his story, with the hope that he could reach out to at least one person who has experienced, or was currently experiencing, similar challenges so that others might know that even in the darkest moments of despair, there is bright sunshine after every thunderstorm if you just don't give up.

Mom: Jeff, what do you think your purpose is in this lifetime?

Jeff: I would say it's to love people, learn how to love people and help them, and I would say I'm doing that in my own way. I mean, I don't do stardom or be on stage or anything like that, but I do help my parents, and I do help my friends Janice and Gordon. And I think even the people I run across at random, I probably help in some way and don't even know it. I think that when I run across people, I try to make it so they feel better after our encounter than before I met them. I think that would probably be what it would be.

Mom: Tell me about the first time you saw the lights, what you call the "dots."

Jeff: I'm gonna say, roughly, I would have been like four, five, or six years old, something like that. And I just saw them, and I still see them today. They haven't changed, and they're ever present, and they're all around me. It doesn't matter whether my eyes are open or closed. I see them constantly, 24/7, and it's like they're multicolored and they're twirling around really, really quickly. They're just with me, no matter where I am. For a while I just thought everybody saw this; I've asked my mom and other people, "Well, don't you see this?" And the answer was no. When I got older, I realized that not everybody does see this, and I'm not sure why they don't. Initially I was afraid of them, but my mom talked to me, and once it was explained to me what they were, I was no longer afraid of the dots. And now I'm glad I've had them with me over the years. I assume they're there to obviously protect me, like on the night of the dog. But maybe they're there for other reasons, too; that I'm not 100 percent sure of. And that does bring me comfort.

Mom: You mentioned the night of the dog. Would you tell us about that?

Jeff: Yeah, it was November of 1999, and I was kinda in the middle of the night in Simi Valley. I was waiting for a Metrolink train, and I was the only one at the station. There was a fence on either side and a dry irrigation channel, or whatever you want to call it. I'm looking on the far side of that channel, on the other side of the fence, and there's this mean junkyard-type dog. I don't know the breed or anything, and it's walking along and, all of a sudden, I'm afraid. I know it's going to come over, and I don't want it to come over. Sure enough, there's a hole in the fence. And it comes through that fence at the hole, down the embankment, and over to my side. It's obviously hungry and mean, and it's like, *g-r-r-r-r*, and I'm just sitting and thinking, "Oh my gosh, I'm gonna die here tonight, and no one's ever gonna know what happened to me. I'm just here by myself." And the dog came;

I don't know exactly how far it was from me, but not real far, and it was like *g-r-r-r-r*, and I'm thinking, "I don't want to die tonight. I still need to be here." So I asked my angels—I didn't specifically ask for a certain one—but I asked them to please protect me from that dog, that I didn't want to die that night. And then it was like a shield of gold just enveloped me, and the dog, with no explanation whatsoever, just quit growling, and it then turned around and left, and it didn't bother me anymore. I mean, it was the strangest thing, and I know I was protected by my angels. Had I not been protected by my angels, I would have been badly hurt or killed.

Mom: Jeff, tell me how it was for you in school.

Jeff: Well, I don't have a whole lot of information about the early, early time. I was at Montessori school, and there was some minor teasing, being made fun of, that the teachers handled. I don't have a real clear memory, but because I was born with cerebral palsy and I walked different, that kinda made me a target for ridicule because kids end up picking on somebody that's different; what they perceive as the weakest person, they're gonna go right for that. I guess they do that to make themselves feel better when, in reality, they're the ones that have the problems because they're having to do this bullying, or whatever you want to call it.

Then I went to a school where I had really good teachers again. But there would be instances when I would be in PE, or whatever, when I couldn't do what the other kids could, and they would ask me, "Why do you walk that way?" or "Why do you walk funny?" Stuff like that. It didn't make me feel good, but I would say, based on the whole spectrum of the years of school, that that was nothing compared to what would happen later on, so I dealt with it as best as I could, and I did have the support of the teachers there, so that was good.

Then we moved to California and I went to a school where some hurtful stuff happened, but it wasn't overly excessive, and I also had the support of the teachers.

The time in middle school really upped the ante. One kid put gum on the bottom of my lock so that I couldn't open it to get into my locker where my books were. They made fun of the way I walked and said stupid stuff, and that didn't feel good.

And then the real problems happened in high school. People were picking on me ruthlessly to the point that one boy even spit on me in class, and it was running down my face. I didn't want to be expelled or anything, so I later asked the teacher how I should handle it, and she didn't really help me, so I talked with the administrator who said I was supposed to run away and tell the principal, but again, they really never did anything about it. They did not put a stop to the awful bullying and what I would call abuse, even though my mom and dad spent so much time there.

I rode my bike to school every day, and one day I was so excited for the school day to end because I had set a goal to accumulate one thousand miles on my odometer, and I knew that I would hit my goal on the way home. My mom and dad knew what that goal meant to me and were really excited for me to achieve it, and we were all going out for ice cream to celebrate my achievement.

After my last class I walked to my bike and found it laying on the ground, and the odometer had been busted. I was so upset because by damaging my odometer, they destroyed my chance of reaching my goal. I loved riding my bike because it made me feel like a normal kid when I was riding it, and it was one way I could compensate for being different.

Also, I recall a boy who licked my ear and then said that I was one of "Jerry's kids." That hurt real bad because I couldn't help the way I walked. Again, I just dealt with everything the best I could. But by November, it was so bad that I couldn't take it anymore, and I had a breakdown and reverted to an infant state. I couldn't remember how to shower; I couldn't remember what day it was. I mean, it was like I had lost my mind, and I didn't know if I would get it back. It was a real scary time.

Then I changed to another school, and unfortunately, even though it was a smaller school, they would still pick on me. They made fun of the way I walked, and they put food in my hair. One girl would drop stuff and have me pick it up and then laugh at me. She'd say she couldn't pick it up because she had a skirt on and *yada, yada, yada*. It just went on and on.

And then I went to a public school for the first time. All I wanted to do was learn, but some of the same stuff happened, and it made me feel so bad. I just didn't understand why people had to do hurtful things. And I had another breakdown when I just couldn't handle the abuse anymore.

Amazingly enough, by twelfth grade, people had matured to a point that they pretty much left me alone. I was lonely and didn't feel that I fit in, but there weren't many real bad things that happened.

And then I got into college, and it wasn't too bad at first. However, the scars from all the years of when they did do all that crap were still with me, so I didn't feel good about myself. I do recall getting sick, and I do recall that they had a cafeteria, and for the first couple of weeks, I couldn't even go have a meal there, and when I finally did go have a meal, I would end up going to the very back of the room and sitting by myself, facing the wall. That's pretty much how I did things. Again, there was no one really making fun of me there, but the terrible scars from all that had gone on before were still with me. So I dealt with that as best I could, but because I was sick a lot, I wasn't able to make the good grades that I should have been able to make, and that made me sad. That bothered me for years. Finally, I realized that it didn't really matter in the scheme of things, but it took me a good number of years to realize that.

Definitely before college and before twelfth grade, I never knew what was coming next. Had I not had the physical problems, I don't think I would have been bothered as much. I guess people get bullied to a certain degree because of looking different or being overweight or whatever, but I think I got hit real often and to a harder degree because I was a lot more different from the average person who went to school. It was very traumatic and very difficult, but I did the best I could, and somehow, I managed to finish and go forward.

Mom: Jeff, you mentioned your bike. You loved that bike, and you were very good at riding it. I think it made you feel really good because it gave you freedom. You were just a boy riding your bike like all the other kids. Is there anything you would like to talk about regarding it?

Jeff: I loved my bike. I felt like everybody else when I was on my bike. I didn't think about being different. I didn't think about not being able to walk like everybody else. It just felt good.

I recall very clearly that I was coming home from school one day when I was in the ninth grade, just riding like I normally would, and there was this construction worker. He was obviously not a nice person, because as I was riding by, he stuck out his foot to deliberately trip me. I fell, and he started laughing. I was bleeding and really cut up because I fell totally flat on the ground, and I remember feeling really helpless because there was no way that I could prevent something like that from happening.

I also recall one time I was riding my bike on Ventura Boulevard, and there was this mean person with what looked like steel knuckles on every finger. He saw me and yelled, "Get back here. I'm coming after you." So I rode as fast as I could to get on the other side of the sidewalk, and he just laughed.

I've had some instances happen where people… let's just say, they were less than kind, and they put me down or tried to physically cause harm to me to maybe make themselves feel better. Maybe they were insecure or just ignorant and mean. Maybe mean people just get a rise out of causing harm to someone who is less able-bodied than themselves. At least it wouldn't happen every time, and I loved riding my bike. I even rode it in a marathon!

Mom: Jeff, was there any particular incident in ninth grade that caused you to leave us for a while?

Jeff: I think it was a build-up of over a few months' period of the relentless bullying. There was a certain group of people that were really just relentless, and obviously, since the teacher just went on teaching as if this were not happening, I had no support there at all. My mom and dad tried to help me as much as they could, and I know it was really, really hard for them, but they couldn't be with me all the time. I was a good student who always got As, and I think that was a threat to some of the kids, so they wanted to bring me down with them. They were going to use anything they could to make sure that I wasn't doing well right along with them. And not only that, but they singled me out because, again, I'm different, and anybody who's different is going to be a real easy target for ridicule and crap like that.

I would say it wasn't just one single event, but it was a culmination, day after day after day of relentless picking on me and bullying and all the stuff they did, and finally it reached a point where I just couldn't handle it anymore. So I had to escape in order to just protect myself so I didn't go totally crazy. It was the only way I could get through all of the horrific stuff that happened. I didn't feel good about myself. I mean, who would with all that was going on? I just felt so helpless.

Mom: Would you like to share any thoughts or feelings that you had when you, as you have said, "retreated from life"?

Jeff: Yes, I was very sad and scared, and suicide did cross my mind numerous times. I cried a lot, and I just thought it was a really heavy load. And I wondered, especially the first time, whether I would ever get better or if it was a permanent condition for the rest of my life. That first time was the scariest and the most traumatic. I just thought, *This is so difficult right now and such a hard struggle.* I became real clingy, and I had to be around my mom and dad constantly. And I wouldn't want to be left alone. It was just a real tough time period. At the same time, I did have some good times with them even though I was sick, if that makes any sense, because I was able to go to work with them, and we would hang out and go to lunch and go for drives. I couldn't understand things, but I was able to have some neat experiences with them.

I'll go ahead and segue to something else. Had it not been for my sickness, especially in ninth grade, I would not have met Janice and Gordon. It was one of those things: I had an instant connection with Janice, and when she took me home for a visit and Gordon came home from work, I also had an instant connection with him. We all got along immediately, and I strongly feel that I have known them before. I consider them to be a second mom and dad, and had I not been sick, I don't know that I would have had the opportunity to run into them. You never know how the universe is going to do it, but I would say that there were some blessings even during the time when I was so sick.

I guess the best way to describe it is when I was going through all that, it was like a storm—a very long, scary thunderstorm. It was a long, long period of that, but eventually those storms pass, and then you're left with bright sunshine in their place. I have seen periods of that, too. I don't think any normal person would ever have to go through this, but with being different, it's just a real struggle. I'm doing better now, but in my teens, it was very turbulent.

I'm always on guard, even now. I have to take care of myself by getting plenty of sleep and getting adequate counseling religiously. I am very dedicated to staying well, and I attribute that to God and the angels who are always with me. All of this, I'm sure, served a purpose, and it was a journey for me to get to where I am now, and hopefully, all of this will help somebody.

Mom: Jeff, is there anything else you would like to share?

Jeff: When I was younger, I envied my so called "normal" peers. I thought it would be really nice if I was like that, too. For the longest time I resented being the one who was so challenged both physically and emotionally. The load was so heavy at times that I honestly didn't know if I could handle it. Mom always says that we all have our stories. Some you can see and some you can't, but we all have them. I guess that's true when you think about it.

Obviously, had I not had physical differences, it would have been easier in school and other situations. I'm not gonna say it would have been real easy, because I think anybody could be subject to bullying, but because of both my physical and emotional challenges, I went through some real scary times. I don't think average people really ever have an experience where they just forget who they are or how to dress and shower or what day it is. I mean, I know that's not normal human behavior, but that's what happened to me, and it was just very scary because I didn't know if I could come back, and if not, what would I do? I didn't know what was happening to me, but I do believe it was the only way I could deal with the awful things that happened. I just had to kind of retreat for survival.

The lingering effects of the low self-esteem from all the years of that going on did not go away, and even to this day, when I'm by myself in a restaurant and some kids come in, I feel myself tense up, and I know that it's remnants from things that happened in my past. There are times when I go to a lab that is totally full of people waiting to get blood drawn, and I find myself breaking into a sweat and feeling like I can't be there. I've gotta get right out of that door and get away. The general public at large still causes quite a bit of anxiety, and I never know when I venture out what will happen. I just wish people could be kind to one another.

Those are just some examples that are left over from all the years of trauma. Maybe someone else has had similar experiences, and maybe they can get help from some of the experiences I have gone through. I guess, if that's the case, then all of this was somehow worth it for some higher good or some better purpose.

What I will say has been a blessing is that I was able to move to a city that I love and that makes me feel like I have come home. Even though it's far from my family and it was really hard to be alone physically, it's something I just had to do, and my mom understood. She also understood that although I was alone physically, I was never alone spiritually, because I always knew the angels were with me. I still saw the brightly colored dots like I've talked about. They would swirl around me constantly, and they still do, even as I'm speaking now.

I also have found some spiritual people who totally accept me. Like me, they see the beauty inside a person and don't focus on the outer shell. They don't care about your differences, so I just find myself being able to talk and laugh with them. It's such a comforting and refreshing environment. I have never really had a spiritual person make fun of me, so I am able to concentrate on the goodness of people. I long for the times I am able to be with them as we share love and acceptance with one another.

I really hope and pray that my story will help at least one person who has or is currently going through dark times. The sun *can* shine through the darkest clouds. Just know that you are never alone.

CPSIA information can be obtained at www.ICGtesting.com
Printed in the USA
LVOW07s0447230114

370516LV00005B/7/P